Praise for

Christian Wisdom on Dialogue as a Habit of the Heart

"A breath of fresh air. This book has the power to change the way we relate to others, from personal relationships to global politics. I look forward to using it in parish settings, couples counseling and adult education. Humble, self-reflective, challenging—a great text!"

—**Carolyne Call**, author, *Spiritually Healthy Divorce: Navigating Disruption with Insight and Hope*

"In a time when we are losing the ability to speak and listen to each other, this book gives us a deeper understanding of the process of dialogue along with the tools to use it. Backman's theological sensibility provides a strong foundation for moving us out of the imprisonment of polarization."

—**Pastor Donald Mackenzie**, coauthor, *Getting to the Heart of Interfaith: The Eye-Opening, Hope-Filled Friendship of a Pastor, a Rabbi and an Imam* and *Religon Gone Astray: What We Found at the Heart of Interfaith*

"Leads us through the often treacherous maze of interpersonal communication with humor, humility and—most importantly—hope…. Reminds us that we are all ultimately at home in the same loving God, who delights both in our individuality and in our efforts—no matter how flawed—to truly listen to and love each other along the way."

—**Kristyn Komarnicki**, editor, *PRISM* magazine (PRISMmagazine.org)

"Challenges our sound-bite culture to abandon partisan diatribes and premeditated monologues and to truly engage one another—especially those whom we may prefer to avoid. We learn not only *why* it is necessary to commit to dialogue, but how to construct an effective, spiritually centered and lasting dialogic relationship."

—**Ethan Vesely-Flad**, editor, *Fellowship* magazine, Fellowship of Reconciliation

"Thought-provoking.... A wonderful primer to help us change our interactions to true connection and solving problems together."

—**Judith H. Katz, EdD**, The Kaleel Jamison Consulting Group, Inc.; coauthor, *Opening Doors to Teamwork and Collaboration: 4 Keys that Change EVERYTHING* and *Be BIG: Step Up, Step Out, Be Bold* (with Frederick A. Miller)

"Provides practical and necessary tools that can help foster meaningful dialogue among individuals and groups. Given our current—and often polarized—society, this is a reflective book for parties who aspire to come to the table and create solutions."

—**Sara Hacala**, author, *Saving Civility: 52 Ways to Tame Rude, Crude and Attitude for a Polite Planet*

Why Can't We Talk?

Christian Wisdom on Dialogue as a Habit of the Heart

JOHN BACKMAN

FOREWORD BY KAY LINDAHL

Walking Together, Finding the Way®

SKYLIGHT PATHS®
PUBLISHING

Woodstock, Vermont

Why Can't We Talk?
Christian Wisdom on Dialogue as a Habit of the Heart

2013 Quality Paperback Edition, First Printing
© 2013 by John Backman
Foreword © 2013 by Kay Lindahl

For information regarding permission to reprint material from this book, please mail or fax your request in writing to SkyLight Paths Publishing, Permissions Department, at the address / fax number listed below, or e-mail your request to permissions@skylightpaths.com.

Library of Congress Cataloging-in-Publication Data

Backman, John.
  Why can't we talk? : Christian wisdom on dialogue as a habit of the heart / John Backman. — Quality pbk. ed.
       p. cm.
  Includes bibliographical references and index.
  ISBN 978-1-59473-443-4 (quality pbk. : alk. paper) 1. Oral communication—Religious aspects—Christianity. 2. Conversation—Religious aspects—Christianity. 3. Dialogue. 4. Apologetics. 5. Spiritual life—Christianity. I. Title.
  BV4597.53.C64B33 2012
  241'.4—dc23

                                  2012036204

10 9 8 7 6 5 4 3 2 1

Manufactured in the United States of America
Cover Design: Jenny Buono
Cover Art: ©iStockphoto.com/mrPliskin

SkyLight Paths Publishing is creating a place where people of different spiritual traditions come together for challenge and inspiration, a place where we can help each other understand the mystery that lies at the heart of our existence.

SkyLight Paths sees both believers and seekers as a community that increasingly transcends traditional boundaries of religion and denomination—people wanting to learn from each other, walking together, finding the way.

SkyLight Paths, "Walking Together, Finding the Way" and colophon are trademarks of LongHill Partners, Inc., registered in the U.S. Patent and Trademark Office.

Walking Together, Finding the Way
Published by SkyLight Paths Publishing
A Division of LongHill Partners, Inc.
Sunset Farm Offices, Route 4, P.O. Box 237
Woodstock, VT 05091
Tel: (802) 457-4000   Fax: (802) 457-4004
www.skylightpaths.com

Contents

∞ FOREWORD

Our society is going through a remarkable period of social change that has led to deep polarization on so many issues. All you have to do is read the newspaper, look at the news, or listen to the radio to notice the discord and lack of dialogue in the public sphere. John's deeply thoughtful book could not come at a better time—we do need to learn how to talk to each other, in the face of our differences.

What is unique about this book is that John takes us on a journey that goes underneath the "how to" of dialogue to the heart of its spiritual dimension—the work of the soul. So many of us have been trained to listen critically, judging what the other is saying, looking for what is wrong with that viewpoint, and then trying to persuade the other to our way of thinking. We have forgotten the value of deep conversation, listening and speaking with respect and seeking understanding. John reminds us that we are spiritual beings called to be in relationship with each other. "When hearts connect, angels sing" (*Anonymous*).

Authentic dialogue takes time and energy, which is countercultural in our fast-paced world with its ever-present use of technology, whether cell phones, texting, computers, watching television, or video games. We have forgotten the art of conversation, how to be truly present with others. John offers many suggestions for reminding us how to engage in deep conversation as well as a host of spiritual practices that prepare us for this work of the heart.

It is a particularly good resource for *intra*faith dialogue, as we learn to talk about the difficult issues that face us within our own traditions. One of the things that I have noticed is that often we start these conversations with the best intentions, knowing that our faith teaches that we are to be in communication. We set up meetings and we listen to each other, and sometimes we even find points of agreement. And yet we go away from these meetings feeling that nothing has really changed. My suspicion is that each person often enters into these dialogues with the unconscious belief that if he or she just talks long enough, the other side will be persuaded to his or her view. It doesn't work that way. The practices and tone of this book show how to enter into these conversations more deeply grounded in the wisdom of our souls.

—Kay Lindahl
  founder, The Listening Center

Talking with the Adversary

"I think George W. Bush is a very good president."

It was the summer of 2004. My sister-in-law Jane and I were lounging on the screened-in porch at our father-in-law's house, and she was (thoughtfully as usual) discussing her views of the presidential race. I do not recall my immediate reaction to her opinion of the president, but I'm sure it was some mix of nausea, horror, and righteous indignation.

Then, in a moment of what must have been God's grace, I saw Jane's statement as something else entirely: an opportunity for dialogue.

This sort of thought does not come naturally—to me or to many others. More often than not, we shy away from those who disagree with us—or we angrily state our opinion and brook no dissent. When discussions actually take place, we spend more time marshaling counterarguments than openly listening. Our vested interests overwhelm what we say and hear.

In all of this, we reflect the world around us. Our culture has precious few Platos to model authentic dialogue. Instead, elected officials are frequently adversarial, seeking to win votes as much as to explore issues. Too many pundits and radio hosts would rather shout than talk.

We hear sound-bite policy ideas repeated until they become conventional wisdom. We hear conventional wisdom repeated until we can't imagine questioning it.

Then, without warning, we run across someone of gentle spirit and a genuinely open heart. It feels as though someone has opened a window and let the spring air in. And we wonder why things can't always be like this.

I believe they can. The power to make it happen rests in our hands—when we live out our lives in God's hands.

It was not the most comfortable context for dialogue. My wife's family enjoys debating politics and religion. Several of them are conservative Christians, Republicans, or both; I am neither. We have endured our share of contentious conversations. On the other hand, Jane consistently communicates her perspectives with gentleness, depth of thought, and love. She knows the power of words; as she often tells her husband, "Words mean things." If anyone could pull this off, she could.

To ensure that we didn't devolve into mindless vitriol, we set some ground rules. She would lay out her thoughts about the president's virtues in an unbroken monologue. Then I would describe his vices in the same way. Neither of us could interrupt the other—at all—not even for questions. Neither of us would attempt to formulate rebuttals while the other was speaking (to the extent we could help it). We would simply listen. In the process, we hoped, we would learn something: if not about The Truth, then certainly about each other.

Quite a few authors have written books on conflict resolution, interfaith dialogue, and similar topics. Many of these books are excellent and deserve attention. Almost without exception, however, they focus on the *process,* whether they describe the tricks of the trade ("*I* statements," listening skills, nonverbal cues, and similar tips) or present case studies of successful dialogues. Either way, it's all about the interpersonal.

But is the interpersonal all there is to dialogue? Does the entire process consist of what we say and do at the table? No. There is much we can do to prepare ourselves before the dialogue ever begins. People of faith, Christians included, have a unique contribution to make here, because the giants of their traditions have pointed to a way of life—the "work of the soul"—that, as it turns out, prepares us for authentic dialogue.

The details of this work vary, depending on the specific approach, but the essential ingredients are much the same. By drawing close to God, acting in concert with God's desires, and practicing the virtues of our faith, we undergo an inner transformation. Our vested interests tend to fall away as we focus our attention and ourselves on God. Moreover, this work of the soul opens us to others. We start to see beyond the things that separate us to the essential humanity we share. With this perspective, we are more inclined to love.

And to dialogue. Having engaged in this work of the soul, we come to the table with a clear mind and an open heart, better equipped to set aside our preconceptions at least for the duration of the dialogue. This gives us the perspective to engage the other person more deeply than we could have otherwise. If both people enter the dialogue in this way, they can work together more productively to build their relationship, explore the truth of the matter—and, maybe, reach consensus on a way forward.

With the challenges we face as human beings, this pursuit of dialogue is important. The future of our relationships, of our houses of worship, even of the planet may depend on it. If we cannot talk openly and civilly about family conflict or matters of faith, let alone climate change or nuclear armament, how can we ever overcome the problems that threaten us all?

Jane and I kept up the dialogue over parts of two days. Neither of us changed the other's mind, but that was beside the point. I gained insight into the "opposition" that I could not have gained any other way. I sensed the attractiveness of what many conservatives perceived as the president's solid principles and decisiveness. Just as important, the conversation set the tone for further discussions. And it drew us closer.

Was it a coincidence that Jane and I had tended our relationships with God for a long time? I doubt it. All those years of inner transformation surely played a role in our openness to each other. St. Paul lists patience, kindness, generosity, gentleness, and self-control as "the fruit of the Spirit" (Galatians 5:22–23). Aren't these precisely the types of traits that equip us for authentic dialogue?

None of this made the dialogue easy. I vividly remember how difficult it was to sit and simply listen to an opposing viewpoint for an extended period. It took a great deal of time and energy to make the dialogue work, especially to keep from interrupting with "But what about …?"

Time and energy, of course, are in short supply these days. And to be sure, not every dialogue takes two days. If we prepare our souls beforehand, however, we will find ourselves readier and more open to embracing dialogue whenever the opportunity presents itself.

The results, from my experience, are more than worth the effort. I believe that when we approach people in this way, we form and deepen relationships more easily. We live in greater harmony with others. We tend less toward anger and more toward compassion and peacemaking, which fosters peace within ourselves. As we practice the virtues of our faith, our character grows more robust, better able to withstand temptation and life's ups and downs. Do these benefits sound familiar? They represent the attitudes of heart to which God calls us. Pursuing dialogue as a habit of the heart, then, helps us to live out our calling as Christians: to live, that is, in love with God and one another.

So there is great value in pursuing the work of the soul, the "way of dialogue" as a habit of the heart. That, in short, is the reason for this book: to describe this way so you may adopt it to live more faithfully— and contribute more powerfully to the conversations that shape our lives together.

This book comes largely from my own experience. I do not cite reams of evidence from formal research to substantiate the claims I'm making. I simply offer you the impact that the practices described here have had on my life—and on the lives of people who have earnestly sought God over the past millennia. The stories of saints like Augustine and Francis of Assisi and Thérèse of Lisieux, not to mention thousands of others, speak volumes about the power of God to transform us from the inside out. That transformation goes on today in the lives of many. Believe me when I say it is worth exploring.

Before we start that exploration, however, we have to take issue with an old, old story.

When You Have to Move the Elephant

Long, long ago, four young blind boys lived in four African villages. As children, each had heard tales of an elephant who lived in the vast jungle that surrounded their homes. But children were not allowed to enter the jungle, so they did not know if the tales were true.

In the year these boys became men, an ancient guide traveled among their villages, as was her custom, gathering them together and leading them into the jungle to meet the elephant. When they reached the giant beast, she led each of them to a different part of it, then asked them to put their hands out gently. As they did, they began to murmur.

"Ah! Just as I have heard. The elephant is like a tree," murmured the young man who touched the leg.

"No, he feels like a snake," said the man who felt the tail.

"Nonsense," argued the man near the ear. "A very large hand fan: that is what he is."

"That is ridiculous," shouted the man near the belly. "He is a giant wall."

They continued to argue until the guide spoke up. "Why are you arguing? All of you are right. Each of you simply touched a different part of the elephant. So the elephant has all the features you mentioned, and even more."

"Ah!" said the young men. Immediately they stopped arguing and were happy again.

Can you spot the flaw in this old story?

Never mind whether African guides really take young men into the jungle for initiation rituals. Forget the likelihood that an elephant would flee, or charge, before the young men approached him. Chalk those up to poetic license.

Instead, take a good long look at the moral. It tells us that we can live in harmony with those who see things differently than we do, if only we accept that we all view reality through the lens of our own experience.

To be sure, it's a wonderful lesson. But real life is so much messier.

The lesson *might* be true if all we had to do was "live and let live." The fact is, people with different, often conflicting perspectives—in a family, a faith community, a workplace, a nation, a world—have to solve problems together. Consider our parable again: What if the elephant suddenly dies and the blind men have to move the body? What if the elephant becomes violent and they must work together to find the best escape route? Suddenly, these men have to talk. More than that, they have to dialogue—to hold their cherished concepts of *elephant* in abeyance, listen carefully to one another, and together discover more of the truth so they can resolve their problem.

This is where we find ourselves today: with many elephants to battle and many decisions to make. Some can change a family's future; some could make or break our planet. All require the concerted effort of people with differing interests and perspectives. And people can only work together when they can *talk* together.

Yet our level of dialogue is not up to the challenge.

That is the imperative of this book: to seek a new way to foster this dialogue—personally, interpersonally, internationally—so we can confront our elephants. Before we start fostering dialogue, however, we have to agree on what it is.

The Elements of Dialogue

As one kind of human communication, dialogue shares many basic elements with its counterparts. It involves at least two people. One person speaks and the others listen. The roles of speaker and listener change every now and then during the communication. The conversation is verbal (or, if via letter or e-mail, written) but often involves nonverbal elements. The participants focus on a particular topic, for however brief a time.

Yet in its aims, its structure, and especially its motivation, dialogue stands apart.

One of my favorite descriptions of dialogue comes from Robert Apatow, a retired professor and eminent dialogist. "The function of dialogue," he writes, "is to bring people together as friends in the shared exploration of the truth of an issue."[1] In this description lie the seeds of what makes dialogue unique—and why it holds such promise for our own lives.

Dialogue is shared. Rather than fight their way to a compromise at best or an impasse at worst, participants actively collaborate with one another to progress toward a common objective: to work out a marital problem, identify the best site for the new town hall, hear God's will for their faith community. To think of it another way, debaters work at cross-purposes and confront each other; dialogists work together and address the issue.

We get a vivid glimpse of this distinction during election years. Watch the candidates debate and you will see a common pattern. The moderator asks one candidate a probing question. The candidate deflects it and goes on to lay out his agenda. The other candidate pokes holes in the agenda—holes that, as often as not, distort her opponent's position—and describes her own plan. There is little listening or shared exploration of each issue's more complex realities. Whether or not this is acceptable debate technique, it is certainly not dialogue.

By contrast, imagine how refreshing it would be to watch a candidate listen to her opponent and then say, "You know, that's a great point. Let's stop to consider that for a moment." This leads directly to our next element of dialogue.

Dialogue explores. Rather than assert the truth of a position, participants ask questions of an issue, consider possible answers, build on one another's insights, and gradually move closer to a shared understanding— or at least a deeper appreciation of one another's perspectives.

Try this sometime: gather a small group of people and present a proposal for them to discuss. Allow them to respond freely with just two rules: every statement must respond to the one before and begin with the word *but.* You will see the discussion go nowhere as every new insight is thwarted; the participants' enthusiasm quickly deflates, and the energy goes out of the room. Now try it again with the same format, only everyone must begin his statement with *and.* Before you know it, the speakers are adding onto one another's ideas quickly and with energy to arrive at a bigger, better vision of the proposal. *That* is much closer to the ideal of dialogue.[2]

Dialogue focuses on truth. Rather than defend a cherished *view* of the truth against all comers, dialogists actively seek to discover the reality of a situation, whether it involves the underlying dynamics of a family crisis or the root causes of a failing health care system. Even if it cannot ultimately capture The Truth (and few dialogues do), the exchange of perspectives allows the dialogists to discover a broader range of perspectives, which may by itself nudge them closer to the truth—or at least to an effective way to address the issue at hand.

My daughter challenges me with this aspect of dialogue all the time. Ever since she was four, she has been able to articulate why she does what she does. A few years ago, as a young adult, she would call us every now and then with a new thought on her life's direction. Sometimes I thought her idea was out in left field, but as she described the thinking behind it—and I tried to listen—I saw that she might have a point. Even more important, only by listening could I start to ask questions that helped her to refine her thinking and explore her plans more deeply. In short, she expanded my perspective on the issue, so that I could help her expand hers. By the end of our discussion, she often had a clearer notion of where she wants to go in her life and the outline of a plan to get there.

Dialogue involves self-transcendence. "In its highest form," writes Apatow, "dialogue challenges us to give up our prejudices and false beliefs and to allow the innate wisdom that all humans have ... to come forth and express itself."[3] Leonard Swidler, a professor of Catholic thought and interreligious dialogue at Temple University, puts it this way: "In dialogue each partner must listen to the other as openly and sympathetically as s/he can in an attempt to understand the other's position as precisely and, as it were, as much from within, as possible."[4]

Easier said than done. Because we cling to our values and beliefs so deeply, dialogue requires a deliberate effort to set aside those attachments in order to truly hear and digest the perspectives of others. Of course, we cannot set aside our attachments unless we know what they are, which is why self-awareness is essential to this process. By recognizing our own perspectives, then holding them in abeyance, we liberate ourselves to approach the others in a dialogue with a clear mind and an open heart. This recognition of the thinking behind one's beliefs and assertions is a cornerstone of the approach of David Bohm, renowned physicist and author of the landmark *On Dialogue*. "This is really something of crucial importance" in a dialogue, Bohm writes, "to be listening and watching, observing, to give attention to the actual process of thought and the order in which it happens, and to watch for its incoherence, where it's not working properly, and so on."[5]

You may have noticed, in the preceding discussion, that one final element of dialogue keeps popping up: *dialogue fosters mutual understanding.* This is a welcome by-product of the process itself: in listening deeply to others' perspectives for the truth they may hold, we almost cannot help but understand our co-participants a little better, grasp the opposing position a bit more clearly, and learn to tolerate a diversity of thought on the issue.

In many areas, mutual understanding might be even more appropriate as a primary goal than truth seeking. Consider interfaith dialogue. It is unlikely that any discourse between, say, Muslims and Christians would result in a consensus on ultimate truth. But that would make the dialogue no less valuable: indeed, the mutual understanding that results could defuse hostility and lead to peacemaking—and how desperately do we need more interfaith peacemaking in the world?

What Dialogue Is Not

In the spirit of contrarians everywhere, we can hone this description by examining what dialogue is *not*.

As we touched on in the previous section, *dialogue is not debate.* In the best form of debate, participants adopt a position, articulate it, and then defend it against criticism. Conducted civilly, this can be a valuable way for listeners to sort through the facts and perspectives on an issue to develop a perspective of their own. The limitation, though, is that by adopting a position, the debaters automatically have a stake in its success or failure, and therefore a vested interest in defending it. In dialogue, as we have seen, participants put aside their vested interests and "reason together" in a common search for truth or deeper mutual understanding.

This difference becomes even clearer in what passes for debate today. The continual shouting and interruption on some talk shows—political and otherwise—is a far cry from the rational adoption and defense of a position, let alone an authentic dialogue. By the end of the broadcast, these programs have generated more confusion than clarity, more heat than light.

Dialogue is not negotiation. Like debate, negotiation has an essential role to play on every scale of human interaction; it is sometimes the most efficient path to dividing the labor in a work project or passing a municipal budget. This is especially true when an issue must be resolved on a strict timetable; dialogue takes time for exploration and reflection, even when a small group is involved. But while the negotiated settlement might pacify all parties for the short term, there is no guarantee that it will solve the underlying problem; for that, they need to agree on what the problem *is*—and their vested interest in their respective positions hinders them from collaborating in any search for truth. Our blind men may settle on a way to move the elephant, but it won't help if, as part of their compromise, they agree that the elephant is like a snake.

Dialogue is not conversation. "In a conversation," Apatow writes, "people express different views on a range of subjects without concern for where the conversation goes."[6] While conversations can dwell on a particular topic for a while, there is no agreed-upon focus and no specific goal in mind; they can meander from topic to topic. Is this a good thing for human beings? Absolutely. Is it dialogue? No. Dialogue has a set purpose—the focused, shared exploration of truth and mutual understanding. As a result, it requires participants to be more intent in listening to the other, more careful in word choice, more reflective in considering the other's perspectives.

This can get interesting when participants have different ideas of what's going on. When my sister-in-law and I decided to engage in dialogue on the virtues and flaws of George W. Bush, we agreed that we would state our positions thoughtfully and without interruption. As I was listening to Jane explain her views of the president, other relatives joined us; one by one, they began interjecting their opinions and criticizing such popular demons as the "liberal media." Suddenly this was no longer a dialogue, but a conversation: we were simply expressing our views, perhaps engaging in some informal debate, casually interjecting a point here and a point there. If Jane had not intervened, we would have had to continue our dialogue at another time; instead, by explaining what we were doing, she invited others into the dialogue as well.

Dialogue is not persuasion. In persuasion (which is related to debate), one person tries to convince the others not only that his point is valid, but that the others should adopt it, too. Think of salespeople hawking a product, ads promoting a brand, or political candidates describing their fitness for public office. Clearly, their role in the discussion has nothing to do with shared exploration.

Dialogue Defined (in a Way)

So what are we left with? For our purposes, any definition of dialogue must cover two basic points. The first is what we *do*. In dialogue, we think together (in the words of dialogue expert William Isaacs);[7] we join together as friends in a shared exploration of truth (in Apatow's words). We engage in an intentional exploration of an issue, with the goal of deepening mutual understanding and, maybe, moving closer to the reality of that issue.

But our definition requires a second part, too: dialogue as something we *are*. As we become the dialogue we seek, we learn to lead with a clear mind and a listening heart. We learn to hold our convictions lightly, if only for the duration of a specific dialogue, so as to hear the other more clearly. Gradually, our instinct becomes to welcome others and their views with curiosity and compassion, not to defend ourselves with arguments and hostility. When dialogue becomes a habit of the heart, we are poised to engage others in specific dialogues at any time, because our souls are already turned in that direction. We hear something disagreeable and think, "How interesting. Tell me how you got there."

What's at Stake Here

Why have I taken half a chapter to define a commonly used word? Because there is so much at stake in getting this right. Consider just a few areas that might change for the better if the participants sought dialogue.

Marriage and relationships. Depending on how you interpret the statistics, some 40 percent of all marriages end in divorce, and lack of communication ranks near the top of the reasons why. So many factors can derail communication, from misunderstood words to nonverbal cues, from a lack of listening to an intense investment in the outcome.

I discovered two of these factors in college—much to my dismay—when I began to have romantic feelings for my closest friend on campus, a woman named Prudence. Being a suave and elegant young blade, I went to her dorm room, told her we needed to talk, and blurted out something like "I'm beginning to have romantic feelings for you." What I really meant, but couldn't quite articulate, was that I wanted to take our friendship to a deeper level of emotional commitment.

She thought I wanted sex.

With that simple misunderstanding, the entire relationship could have come apart right then and there. It didn't help that another factor impeded our dialogue as well: we were both terrified of the outcome. With Prudence frightened that I was going to pressure her for a *physical* commitment, and I in abject terror that I would lose her, we could not articulate as clearly as we might have otherwise. Only much later were we able to relax and explore the relationship together.

How? By agreeing *not* to define it with a label. In doing so, we set aside the loaded words *friendship* and *dating,* which took some of the thunder out of the discussion. That, in turn, freed us to explore—mutually and with a clearer head—what the relationship might look like in the future. (Apparently it worked; we've been married more than thirty years.)

So often, the emotional investment in a particular position or result forces couples to work against each other, rather than working together to explore the issue. So often, innocuous words and phrases can throw us off course, because we all bring our own experiences and perspectives to our common language. When communication goes awry like that, it becomes difficult and painful, and we find it all too easy to either explode in anger or retreat into silence. Certain topics become off-limits, and our ability to share with our loved ones becomes hampered. Relationships suffer and often fail.

Clearly, there is a lot at stake. By turning to dialogue as a habit of the heart, we give ourselves the emotional latitude to work together and build more fruitful relationships.

Business and the workplace. Here power enters the fray. The status (or potential loss) of one's job, by automatically conferring an emotional stake in any workplace conversation, colors one's relationships. No wonder we see so many yes-people surrounding corporate executives: it is much safer—and more advantageous to one's position—to agree with the boss than to openly disagree. And this despite the fact that open disagreement and dialogue could set the company on a wiser course.

Yet the push for dialogue cannot come from just anyone in an organization. It would take extraordinary courage for a midlevel employee, or even a junior executive, to consistently ask the honest questions and probe the sacred cows that dialogue requires. Because of the power relationships in play, then, a culture of openness and dialogue must come from the top, or at least with official sanction from the top.

When it does, good things can happen. Every month, senior leaders of one company meet with small groups of the rank and file for an hour, not just to discuss company initiatives but to hear their concerns. Thanks to the feedback from those meetings, workers on every shift now have access to company-sponsored child care, a key contributor to employee satisfaction. In another initiative, the company gives cash incentives to small groups of employees who meet to discuss and propose solutions to problems in their immediate area. Without this kind of input, senior executives would have no way of even knowing there was a problem; because they listen and encourage dialogue, they have a more efficient company and a more loyal workforce.

Examples like this will sound familiar to practitioners of inclusion and organization development. In their book *The Inclusion Breakthrough: Unleashing the Real Power of Diversity*, Frederick A. Miller and Judith H. Katz tout the power of inclusion to bring a 360-degree perspective to each organizational situation or issue. When *everyone* in an organization is heard and valued, from the CEO to the machinist on the third shift, new insights arise that may never have come to light before—and the resulting breadth of vision can lead to better solutions and smarter decisions. Moreover, being heard encourages people to speak up, to hear others, and to collaborate on solutions. The principles of dialogue, both as a practice of attentive listening and as a habit of the heart, can contribute substantially to the process of making this dynamic part of any organization.[8]

In a world of continual change and ever-increasing speed, accessing this 360-degree vision can make the difference between excellence and mediocrity or even success and failure. Here, too, the stakes for dialogue are high indeed.

Communities of faith. Take one look at the worldwide Anglican Communion (and its U.S. expression, the Episcopal Church) and you will quickly grasp the stakes in faith traditions—and the challenges they face in dialoguing across divides.

For decades, Anglican leaders have made attempts to talk through their differences over human sexuality. The twentieth century's last three Lambeth conferences—the decennial gatherings of the world's

Anglican bishops to address doctrine and other issues—called for a process of listening to one another on the topic of homosexuality. Has this process taken place? Yes and no. The last thirty years have seen some inspiring examples of dialogue on the issue—notably an annual gathering of Anglican primates (the heads of national churches) facilitated by the Public Conversations Project from 1998 to 2001.[9] One participant sounded a note of hope typical of many successful dialogues: "While our differences remain, the relationships between us have been strengthened and deepened."

On a broader scale, however, others in the Anglican Communion see little progress. "According to Gregory Cameron of the Anglican Communion Office, 'nothing happened' in regard to this process until quite recently. According to Gene Robinson ... the Listening Process 'is a myth.'"[10] Particularly since the ordination of Robinson (an openly gay man in a long-term relationship) as bishop of New Hampshire in 2003, too much "dialogue" has consisted of restatements of positions and procedural moves to push for some final decision. Many on both sides of the issue have tired of the conversation, and some wish that the "other side" would just go away.

Now consider that this is only one small denomination in one period of history. These disputes and strained relationships have taken place in nearly all faith traditions for as long as humanity has practiced religion. Each time it occurs, nonpractitioners look at the dissension, pronounce the factions just as imperfect as the rest of humanity, and conclude (erroneously) that their message has no relevance for resolving the world's pressing issues. While this is hardly the sole reason why attendance at mainline U.S. churches has declined dramatically, it surely doesn't help.

Dialogue does not always resolve differences; some are simply irreconcilable. Yet even when they are, authentic dialogue can help us develop respect for one another while still (amicably) disagreeing. In the process, the connections we foster enable us to continue our work together as our institutions fracture. If the Anglican Communion were to divide in two, why wouldn't we work with believers on the "other side" to bring health care and education to the world's poorest peoples? Without dialogue, the risk is great that we will part bitterly, sever our relationships, and prevent ourselves from working hand in hand to move the elephants that threaten us all.

National issues and global dilemmas. Dialogue is crucial to some public issues because, by definition, there is no other way to resolve them. In a world that has one biosphere and many national borders, any solution to the problem of climate change must include as many nations as possible, and certainly *all* nations that make a significant impact on the environment. The major limitation of the Kyoto Protocol, which admirably prescribed substantial cuts in emissions levels, was that it did not include two of the world's largest economies and polluters—China and India. Dialogue with *everyone* at the table might have enabled some version of Kyoto that made the necessary cuts while addressing the needs of emerging nations to develop their economies.

This interconnectedness isn't limited to issues of nature. If the 2008 meltdown in subprime mortgages and investment banks taught us anything, it is that nearly every part of global finance is inextricably linked to nearly every other part. Otherwise, a slump in the U.S. real estate market would not have brought Iceland to the brink of bankruptcy, Asian stock markets would not have suffered triple-digit losses because of the news, and the Dow, reacting to Asia's reaction to the United States, would not have followed suit. The recent crisis in the euro zone carries the same lesson. It has often been said that when America sneezes, the world catches cold; now many regions of the world can be Typhoid Mary or her victim. Because of this, actions to right the global financial ship must include *all* relevant regions. Dialogue can help them coordinate their action.

And what of war and peace? Because of the enormously high stakes involved, one nation-state cannot unilaterally lay down its nuclear weapons; only when rivals agree mutually to deactivate their arsenals can these weapons be eliminated. Similarly, unilateral action by many players on the world stage, from regional strategic alliances to the parties in a border dispute, could destabilize large swaths of the globe.

To be sure, many forms of communication prove useful in resolving the complex issues of war and peace. Negotiation will always play a primary role, particularly in the resolution of details. Persuasion may well bring about compromises. But one deeper issue among nations provides a unique role for dialogue: a profound loss of trust in the "other side." This mistrust pervades some of the world's most intractable conflicts, such as the Israeli-Palestinian struggle, the dispute over Kashmir, or the tension between Islam and the West. The two sides will hardly persuade one another of anything; the suspicion of hidden agendas prevents it. Negotiation can only be effective if the parties share some common ground, and many do not. In these most irreconcilable of situations, authentic dialogue—with its unique power to refocus the participants, clear the mind, and introduce mutuality—may be the only way to make any progress at all.

No Talk, No Peace

So dialogue just might help us work through a whole raft of issues, both personal and international. And yet consider the failures we see in many of the conflicts discussed above (and elsewhere in this book). Decades of negotiation between Israel and Palestinian organizations have not stopped the killing. Too many Americans remain woefully ignorant of, and suspicious of, Islam. Many couples simply cannot find a way to understand each other.

In short, we are woefully ill-equipped to take on world-threatening (or even relationship-threatening) issues, because we have lost the ability to dialogue. Take a look at what passes for public discourse these days. For hours every day, on hundreds of stations across the United States, talk radio seethes with righteous anger and simplistic claims about the "other side." On the nightly news (and anytime online), government leaders use carefully crafted phrases to distort the other side's positions and beliefs while promoting their own. Advertisers seek new ways to saturate the marketplace with persuasion, which is why we now see ads on sidewalks, in public restrooms, and even on the occasional cow.[11] The cumulative effect of thousands of companies conveying thousands of messages can become so cacophonous that it shuts out rational thought. Many television characters are too emotionally bankrupt to hold an honest conversation, let alone serve as models of dialogue and collaboration.

Our celebrities and sports heroes more often repeat the same old clichés than offer refreshing insight.

Whether we willingly expose ourselves to these messages or not, they are inextricably woven into our culture. Without a conscious effort to engage in authentic dialogue, they become part of our DNA—and thus put us at a disadvantage when embarking on our own attempts at communication.

Tragically, the pervasive loss of dialogue exacerbates a loss of trust. We no longer trust what our elected leaders say or the claims of advertisers. In fact, we *assume* they are distorting the truth. And yet without this trust, as we discussed earlier, no relationship—interpersonal or international—can move forward to full flower.

Instead, we move in one of three directions. The first is a tendency toward violence, whether physical or otherwise. If you can't talk your way through conflicts, violence presents itself as a tempting alternative. It may be one reason why family discussions on sensitive topics escalate into shouting matches, and sometimes worse. It may motivate those who take part in riots, whether they be urban dwellers in Detroit during the 1960s or victims of food shortages in one of the world's poorest nations. If your situation is desperate and you're not being heard, you might think that smashing store windows will send a message to those in power.

The second direction is the spiritual impoverishment that stems from avoiding conflict at all costs. In the name of "being nice," we go out of our way to avoid delicate topics. Think of the old saw about the two subjects you should never discuss: politics and religion. Why not discuss them? Because we don't know how to communicate on such sensitive topics without devolving into anger and, possibly, violence.

Advertising, for all its claims to edginess, often falls into blandspeak to avoid presenting a "negative" message or offending a part of the audience. I have sat in meetings where even the word *not* in an ad drew objections for being negative. I once had a before-and-after concept for a TV commercial shot down because the "before" part could reflect negatively on the overall message.

On a cultural level, I see this striving for niceness spawning an ironic and curious countertrend: a tendency toward wildly offensive expressions, as in the routines of some modern comedians. It was no accident, I think, that the rise of "politically correct" speech came along right around the time that comedians who laced their routines with racial and gender epithets became popular.

This is *not* an excuse for the use of words that historically have been used to alienate and oppress various identity groups. The point is simply that excessive niceness and hypersensitivity have the power to stifle authentic dialogue—which, left to its own devices, can foster the very sensitivity that "nice folks" seek. What better way to understand why certain terms are offensive than to dialogue with the people whom they offend?

The third direction involves force-fitting relationships by "getting everything in writing." Marriage in the twenty-first century—ostensibly one of our culture's deepest expressions of trust—often begins with a prenuptial agreement. Many contracts attempt to specify every aspect of a business relationship in black and white. On a practical level, it is difficult to argue for a world without contracts; they are invaluable for clearing up misunderstandings, providing a framework for relationships, and protecting the parties thereto in a frighteningly litigious society. It is the obsession with putting *everything* in formal agreements that both bespeaks and perpetuates an ongoing loss of trust.

For evidence that this is the case, listen carefully as people pontificate about these developments. Those of a certain age might bemoan the need for prenups in today's society. Businesspeople wax nostalgic for the "handshake deal" and a time when "your word was your bond." What you will hear, beneath the words, is a yearning for trust—the kind of trust that dialogue is well suited to grow.

So what are we left with? A loss of trust, a loss of authentic dialogue, and an alternative—the "shouting model"—that has moved us no closer to resolution of the issues that confront us. In many cases, progress is made only through the bluntest of instruments, such as legislation and the courts.

There is a better way. By preparing ourselves to live out dialogue as a habit of the heart, we also clear the path to restoring trust and moving forward together. It is time to see the stakes for what they are—and put our hearts to the task of learning this way.

FOR YOUR CONSIDERATION ...

1. How has this chapter changed or enriched your understanding of dialogue?

2. How do you seek to promote dialogue in your own life? In what areas of your life does dialogue happen most naturally for you? Where do you find it a struggle?

3. With what in this chapter do you disagree? Why?

Hearing the Call
to Dialogue

What would Jesus do about dialogue?

We've seen the urgent need for dialogue in ourselves, our relationships, and our world. That alone is reason enough to pursue it. Even so, as Christians, we live our lives in response to a more specific call: a "divine nudge" to live like Christ and follow his teachings. That call can be found not only in the needs of the world, but also in the tradition of the Church, the depths of our hearts, and the pages of scripture. A closer look at this last source, especially, can give us a deeper understanding of what we are called *to*.

Peace and Love and the Children of God

The word *dialogue* appears almost nowhere in the Bible. It shows up in one or two translations, but not in the sense we're discussing here. Yet dialogue is not an end in itself, but a means to even more important ends—and the Bible waxes eloquent about those ends.

Two of them get explicit expression in the Sermon on the Mount, perhaps Jesus's most sweeping single statement of his approach to faith.

Blessed are the peacemakers, for they will be called children of God.

(MATTHEW 5:8)

You have heard that it was said, "You shall love your neighbor and hate your enemy." But I say to you, Love your enemies and pray for those who persecute you, so that you may be children of your Father in heaven.

(MATTHEW 5:43–45A)

The yearning for peace runs throughout the pages of scripture. Moses's famous benediction, which God gave him to bless the people of Israel, ends with peace: "The Lord bless you and keep you; the Lord make his face to shine upon you, and be gracious to you; the Lord lift up his countenance upon you, and give you peace" (Numbers 6:22–26). The prophet Jeremiah castigates the leaders of Israel for proclaiming a superficial peace as the real thing: "They have treated the wound of my people carelessly, saying, 'Peace, peace,' when there is no peace" (Jeremiah 6:14, 8:11). The psalmist expresses one of the deepest desires of the human spirit: "May the Lord bless his people with peace!" (Psalm 29:11).

Why is peace so important? Yes, it *feels* better than war or conflict (to many people, at least), but what makes it better? A large part of peace's importance, I believe, comes from its status as the foundation of most things human. Without inner peace, it is difficult to be our best selves in the world, to produce all the fruit we are capable of producing. If you have ever wrestled with an emotional illness or lived through an ongoing crisis, you know how difficult it is to write a story, or solve an engineering problem, or participate fully in a workgroup on one of your bad days. Yes, people sometimes rise to the occasion in acute crisis situations. Over the course of months and years, however, living abundantly from a position of turmoil can be extraordinarily difficult. Among the few who do it well, how many have found some center of peace and strength from which to persevere through the crisis?

If peace is fundamental to human life, love is even more funda-mental to the pages of scripture. In his call to "love your enemies"—as in so many other sections of the Sermon on the Mount—Jesus pushes beyond the command of the Mosaic Law to an even more rigorous observance. Neither do the Gospels stop there: it is one thing to "pray for those who persecute you," something else again to follow Jesus's command to "love one another as I have loved you" (John 13:34)—especially when that love extends to laying down one's life for the other. Jesus speaks of love as the sum of "all the law and the prophets" (Matthew 22:40).

Now go back to our original quotes from the Sermon on the Mount. Notice that the promise is the same: by making peace, by loving our enemies, we are children of God. The phrase also shows up in an oft-quoted passage from the Gospel of John: "To all who received [Christ], who believed in his name, he gave power to become children of God, who were born, not of blood or of the will of the flesh or of the will of [humanity], but of God" (John 1:12–13).

What does this mean? It speaks, I think, not of mere familial relations but rather of affinity. To be a child of God is to reflect God's own charac-ter. In the words of the medieval mystic Meister Eckhart, "If you are to be a child of God, you cannot be one unless you have God's very being."[1] Children of God, out of their deep connection to the Divine, mirror God's orientation toward the world. So if people who reflect God are peacemak-ers committed to love, so God must be as well. If peace and love mark us as children of God, they must reside in God's heart, too.

Of course, the scriptures testify directly to this. The single most fun-damental statement about the essence of God, I believe, is the famous statement from the First Letter of John: "God is love" (1 John 4:8). The apostle Paul often refers to God as the "God of peace." And his beloved list of the "fruit of the Spirit"—by which, according to the words of Jesus in Matthew, we will know the children of God (Matthew 7:15–20)—begins with love, joy, and peace (Galatians 5:22–23).

But *how* do we make peace? *How* do we love in a way that matters? Certainly we can do so from afar. Praying for people halfway around the world is a loving act. So is making a contribution to alleviate poverty and disease. But even in these acts, we can love people so much more effectively when we know them. You can pray for the people of sub-Saharan Africa in a general way, but how much more specifically can you pray or donate when you know that they need mosquito nets to reduce the incidence of malaria or that women are starting their own businesses to get out of poverty?

This is even truer when the love is concrete and hands-on. I can see you're having a bad day and pray for you from afar. If, however, I know that your parents are ill or you're struggling with a midlife crisis or have issues at work, not only can I pray more concretely, but I can be available to you as a sounding board. I can help you think through a specific problem from within your perspective, because I *know* you and what you're struggling with. This operates on an international level, too. Think of all the development and disaster relief efforts that foundered because the organizations behind them used their own methods—ideal for their own conditions—without taking the time to listen, learn, and act according to local circumstances.

To put it simply, how can I act in your best interests, support you most effectively as a friend, look out for your greatest good, unless I know you? How can I know you unless I listen to you? This is where dialogue looms large: because it involves listening on an intentionally deep and attentive level, it provides an extraordinarily effective route to knowing—and hence loving—the other.

Love defines us. Peace is a cornerstone of a fruitful life. God cares deeply about both. Dialogue fosters them.

The Example of Jesus

You might find it odd to think of Jesus's life and ministry as promoting dialogue, and with good reason. His mission was to proclaim a message and to act in the world. That means more talking than listening, and the Gospels tell us that Jesus did a lot of proclaiming. Every now and then, however, these same Gospels record a story in which Jesus showed a capacity for listening and for being surprised, which happens often in dialogue. It is even possible that these "points of listening" shaped Jesus's understanding of his mission and ministry.

Early in Luke's Gospel, a Roman centurion (the overseer of one hundred soldiers in the Roman army) is grieving over a beloved slave with a serious illness. Getting wind of the itinerant healing rabbi coming through his area, he sends Jewish elders to tell Jesus his story and vouch for him as a true friend of Israel. When Jesus heads toward his home, however, the centurion hurriedly sends friends to stop him with words that echo the prayer just before Communion in the Roman Catholic Mass: "Lord, do not trouble yourself, for I am not worthy to have you come under my roof; therefore I did not presume to come to you. But only speak the word, and let my servant be healed" (Luke 7:6–7). Jesus is amazed, and one can imagine his cognitive dissonance. *A Roman? With this degree of faith? Isn't my mission specifically to the house of Israel? What am I to make of this?* Moved by the centurion's faith, he heals the slave "from a distance," and "when those who had been sent returned to the house, they found the slave in good health" (Luke 7:10).

This theme crops up again later in the Gospel narrative.[2] Jesus travels to the region of Tyre and Sidon (a curious move for someone with a mission to Israel, since the region was "largely gentile and despised by Jews").[3] A Canaanite woman asks him to cast the demon out of her daughter. He demurs by quoting his mission—"I was sent only to the lost sheep of the house of Israel"—and adds the quote that, at least to postmodern minds, is one of the most disturbing in the Gospels: "It is not fair to take the children's food [i.e., the message intended for Israel] and throw it to the dogs [i.e., Gentiles]." Undeterred by being called a "dog," she parries with "Yes, Lord, yet even the dogs eat the crumbs that fall from their masters' table." Again, Jesus is confronted with the inner orientation he is trying to foster (great faith) in someone to whom, in his view, he is not called. Did these two encounters teach him something, expand his vision of the world, and set the stage for the inclusion of the Gentiles in the book of Acts?

Not long thereafter, Jesus asks his famous question. Mark's Gospel puts it most directly: "Who do people say that I am?" (8:27). I have often heard this passage (like the story of the Canaanite woman cited above) interpreted as Jesus's testing the people before him—gauging the depth of their faith and understanding. But the ruminations of author and editor Cullen Murphy in *The Atlantic* have always haunted me:

This is one of the most resonant questions in the whole of the New Testament. It is the question, it seems, of a man who wishes to disturb but who is also himself disturbed; of a man who has somehow found himself in deeper waters than anticipated; of a man at once baffled and intrigued by a destiny that he may have begun to glimpse but of which he is not fully aware. And thus, seeking guidance, seeking perhaps to ken the range of possibilities, Jesus put the question to his followers. It is an affecting and very human moment.[4]

To be sure, Jesus had a message to deliver and a "primary audience" to deliver it to. He talked a *lot:* telling stories, giving sermons, debating the meaning of the Law of Moses. But as these few accounts tell us, he also had a capacity to hear, to be amazed by what he heard, and to let it shape his thinking. These are the most basic elements of dialogue, and we do well to take them as an example.

The Example of the "Other Jesus"

On the other hand, the Gospels also present a very different side of Jesus, especially in regard to peacemaking. He continually clashes with the religious authorities of his time. He upbraids his disciples, sometimes vehemently, for their lack of faith and understanding. He overturns the tables of the moneychangers who ply their trade at the Temple in Jerusalem. And at one point (Matthew 10:34–36), he describes his mission as something quite different:

> Do not think that I have come to bring peace to the earth; I have not come to bring peace, but a sword. For I have come to set a man against his father, and a daughter against her mother, and a daughter-in-law against her mother-in-law; and one's foes will be members of one's own household.

What's happening here? To answer in depth, let's look at a common misconception of peacemaking—and of Jesus. Our Christian collective unconscious includes many images that fit into the category of "gentle Jesus, meek and mild."[5] Many people regard peacemaking and compassion as "soft" values, having to do with the avoidance of conflict. According to this line of thinking, anyone who compromises belongs to the "muddled middle," and people who cherish the pursuit of compassion lack conviction.

The Jesus of the Gospels puts that thinking to rest. His message, by its very nature, poses a challenge to his era's status quo. His vision of the kingdom of God, which stands at the center of the Gospel, calls the religious hierarchy of his day away from an exclusive focus on rigid observances and back to the "weightier matters of the law: justice and mercy and faith" (Matthew 23:23). As he practices this approach to faith—healing on the Sabbath; dining with the most reviled members of society; insisting that what comes from our heart, and not what goes into the stomach, makes us unclean—the religious leaders see him as a threat.

The *sword* passage, I believe, is describing precisely this dynamic. Jesus is not actively encouraging his followers to schism and violence. He is, rather, pointing out that his message will inevitably bring conflict.

So it is with us. We can seek peace and exercise compassion with people even while carrying a message that will upset them. Moreover, as in Jesus's example, the very message of peace and compassion will upset people; it calls them to look into their own hearts and to change. If anything, dialogue becomes *more* valuable in situations like these, because it is a way to navigate the conflict and pursue the compassion that Jesus seeks to bring to the world.

Paul and Dialogue

Like Jesus, the Paul of the Christian Scriptures does not engage specifically in the type of dialogue we are exploring here. His mission, too, was to spread the good news of Jesus rather than to "think together" with others to achieve greater clarity or the resolution of an issue. Still, in certain situations, his approach resembles the spirit of dialogue.

Consider his time in Athens (Acts 17:16–33). Ironically, the author of Acts describes the city itself as a center of dialogue: "Now all the Athenians and the foreigners living there would spend their time in nothing but telling or hearing something new."[6] Some of them greet Paul with a statement that could have come straight out of a how-to-dialogue manual: "May we know what this new teaching is that you are presenting? It sounds rather strange to us, so we would like to know what it means." The curiosity expressed here is a hallmark of the orientation of heart and mind that is supremely conducive to authentic dialogue.

Paul sees an opportunity to proclaim the Gospel. His response, to be clear, is *not* dialogue, because it is aimed at persuasion. Even so, it makes use of tactics that are indeed dialogic:

- He respects and affirms the religious impulse of his audience: "Athenians, I see how extremely religious you are in every way."

- He links to their ideas to make his point: "As I went through the city and looked carefully at the objects of your worship, I found among them an altar with the inscription, 'To an unknown God.' What therefore you worship as unknown, this I proclaim to you."

- He quotes Athenian thinkers to establish common ground: "For 'In him we live and move and have our being'; as even some of your own poets have said, 'For we too are his offspring.'"

It is easy to imagine a more confrontational approach. Paul could have condemned the Athenians for their practices; he could have threatened them with hell. More to the point, he *could* have given voice to his gut reaction: "While Paul was waiting … in Athens, he was deeply distressed to see that the city was full of idols." Instead, rather than preaching *at* the Athenians, treating them and their religion as inferior, he presents his argument *to* them—not countenancing their idols but rather affirming common ground while making his point. As a result, he has about as much impact as we might expect in the situation: "Some scoffed; but others said, 'We will hear you again about this.'… But some of them joined him and became believers."

This kind of experience was not unusual for Paul, at least if another passage from his writings is any indication. In his First Letter to the Corinthians (9:19–23), he outlines his approach to encounters outside the Christian community, and it sounds very much like what happened in Athens:

For though I am free with respect to all, I have made myself a slave to all, so that I might win more of them. To the Jews I became as a Jew, in order to win Jews. To those under the law I became as one under the law (though I myself am not under the law), so that I might win those under the law. To those outside the law I became as one outside the law (though I am … under Christ's law), so that I might win those outside the law. To the weak I became weak, so that I might win the weak. I have become all things to all people, that I might by all means save some.

Again, Paul's mission was not dialogue; it was evangelism. But one can make the case that, given the ongoing call to evangelism that the Church hears in Jesus's Great Commission (Matthew 28:18–20), this approach holds a great deal of relevance to the conditions of our age. In chapter 9, we will look more closely at this issue and how taking it one step further—into dialogue *as* evangelism—makes sense for a postmodern world.

That We May All Be One

Last words fascinate us. Particularly in the case of sages and holy people, we often hope to hear one last nugget of wisdom, one climactic statement, a "takeaway" that we can understand and live by.

Jesus's final discourse and prayer in the Gospel of John (chapters 13–17) have that flavor. Knowing the danger he faces, aware that his death is imminent, he lays out a vision for the life his disciples will face— and the way they should live—after he leaves them. Instructions like that are not given lightly. No wonder they are so often quoted and touted among Jesus's most essential sayings.

So what does Jesus say? He sets a new standard for love, as we have seen (John 13:34). He describes the coming relationship between the disciples and the Holy Spirit. He emphasizes that following his message *will* bring conflict with the world. Loving, inspired, prophetic: words that could, indeed should, describe the Church in any age.

But there is another such word, and Jesus expresses it most eloquently in the prayer that follows his discourse (John 17:20–23):

I ask not only on behalf of these [his disciples at the time], but also on behalf of those who will believe in me through their word, that they may all be one. As you, Father, are in me and I am in you, may they also be one in us, so that the world may believe that you have sent me. The glory that you have given me I have given them, so that they may be one, as we are one, I in them and you in me, that they may become completely one.

As we discussed in chapter 1, the Church has a checkered history when it comes to unity. The profusion of Christian denominations, many of which came into being in the wake of schism, provides ample testimony to that. We have already seen how the decades-old fight over same-sex relationships has spawned the ardent wish that the "other side" would just go away. The same wish was also expressed during the conflict over women's ordination. Unity is an underappreciated virtue.

To be sure, not every relationship works out. That goes for groups as well as individuals. Irreconcilable differences are, well, irreconcilable, and often excruciating. The people involved in any breakup or schism—on every side—need abundant love and grace.

Still, the dream of Jesus was for something else: a oneness of spirit and mutual love that inspired people to persevere with one another, for as long as humanly possible, and in doing so serve as the best and highest proof of the extravagant love of God. By definition, this oneness—or at least its manifestation in the world—requires deep, abiding relationships. And relationships grow through dialogue.

The Call to Dialogue in the Real World

Dialogue, then, can be invaluable in advancing qualities of life that are close to the heart of God. Through the pursuit of dialogue, we can engage in peacemaking, cultivate love, and lay the groundwork for unity. We can take heart from the examples of Jesus and Paul as they not only preached but listened to those around them.

So why aren't we doing this? Partly because there are many roadblocks in our way—and they are as much a part of life in the twenty-first century as the air we breathe. It is to those roadblocks that we now turn our attention.

FOR YOUR CONSIDERATION ...

1. How do you see the future of the Church, particularly with regard to the controversies that currently divide it? Can we still preserve the unity to which Jesus calls us, and if so, how?

2. How do you see the future of *your* church or denomination?

3. Could you be a catalyst for change or reconciliation in the issues that divide the Church (or your church)? How? What gifts do you have that would lend themselves to this type of effort?

4. Some of the scripture passages quoted in this chapter—like the story of the Canaanite woman, or *I have not come to bring peace, but a sword*—are difficult for many of us. How do you interpret them? How does your thinking connect to the broader mission of Jesus?

5. With what in this chapter do you disagree? Why?

Roadblocks on the Way

W hat's wrong with us, anyway? Why *can't* we talk? Why do we fail to listen and refuse to budge while the world's most pressing problems threaten to overwhelm us? If dialogue holds such potential for our relationships and our world, what in the world is stopping us?

It would be lovely to think that we just lack the training. If that were true, a few well-crafted workshops, some how-to books, and sufficient media exposure would put us all on the same page. Alas, our lack of dialogue springs from much deeper currents within our culture. Some of them have shaped the social landscape in ways that make the nightly news; others seem so innocuous that their effect on dialogue is startling. Let's look at six of these roadblocks and see how they keep us from talking.

Right There in Black and White

My friend came up to me with fire in her eyes. "I want to hear that you will *not* vote for *anything less* than full reproductive rights for women," she spat out.

I had never seen her quite like this. Yes, she holds strong convictions, but she tends more toward ironic and wickedly funny than out-and-out angry. Still, she knew I was a voting member of a decision-making body, and a proposal related to abortion was on the floor for consideration. She wanted to hear that I would brook no compromise, and she was not in a mood to entertain other perspectives.

Black or white. All or nothing. I've caught myself thinking this way a lot over the years. Perhaps everyone does it at one time or another, in one situation or another. And surely we see it in society at large. Many people of faith view their scriptures as true and accurate in every detail.[1] Idealists have gone to extraordinary lengths to create a "pure" society, using a rigid definition of that term. Millions of people embrace a "my country, right or wrong, love it or leave it" form of nationalism.

Some people have done a great deal of good by acting on their absolute convictions. Others have wreaked unimaginable evil: the hard-line Communist leaders of the twentieth century—Stalin, Mao, Pol Pot—brooked little if any dissent as they slaughtered millions. Most people fall somewhere in between. The issue, for our purposes, is not the morality, validity, or effectiveness of absolute thinking, but rather the fact that it makes dialogue extraordinarily difficult.

This is not illogical. If you are certain that your belief is the absolute truth, why dialogue with anyone who disagrees with it? Indeed, by doing so, you may be tempted to consider ideas that run contrary to yours. No wonder some subcultures with absolute belief systems warn their adherents against engaging people with contrary ideas. I remember hearing this as a brand-new Christian with absolute beliefs: conversations about other faiths or spiritual practices were seen as "giving the devil an opening."

To see how a belief in absolutes works in real life, look at the debate in Christendom over same-sex marriage. Some half-dozen Bible passages could be construed as prohibiting sexual relations between two members of the same gender; at least three of them are (or appear to be) explicit.[2] Those who believe that "the Bible is without error or fault in all its teaching" take these passages literally, as true for all time. Many arguments to the contrary—for instance, that the passage may be referring not to committed same-sex relationships but to temple prostitution, which was common when the passage was written—are seen as attempts to gloss over the "plain truth, right there in black and white." Again, if the plain truth is evident, why dialogue about it with those who disagree?

It would be one thing if absolute beliefs began and ended with a circumscribed set of truth, like the actual words of a holy book. Often, however, the circle of "absolute truth" widens to include interpretations, placing even more topics off-limits for dialogue and into the realm of controversy and contention. The debate in the United States about the beginning and end of life is a classic example. While the Bible does not mention abortion or euthanasia by name, many conservative Christians oppose both as a logical conclusion from God's creation of (and therefore sovereignty over) all of life. "As Christians and Jews, we are not authorized ... to cut short the years that God gives to us or others," wrote a group of distinguished religious thinkers in a discussion of euthanasia.[3]

It is a simple step from absolute statements like the quotation above to absolute thinking on associated issues. As a result, we get unyielding opposition to embryonic stem cell research on the grounds that God's gift of life begins right at conception and therefore must be preserved at all costs, even when the embryos have been created for research. At the other end of life, we get the Terri Schiavo affair—during which, in 2005, federal legislators lined up to keep the young Florida woman alive after fifteen years of living in what state courts called a "persistent vegetative state."[4]

Again, this is not to say that opposition to abortion and euthanasia is necessarily illegitimate. Some very thoughtful people have expressed reservations about both. Indeed, these two issues could benefit from a great deal of attentive listening and authentic dialogue. But the key word in the phrase *unyielding opposition* is *unyielding*. With the certainty of our convictions, we have no reason to bend—or to dialogue with those on the "other side." The more issues and situations we approach in black and white, the fewer the opportunities to bridge our divides and work together to confront the elephants before us.

It's the Media's Fault

This section is not what you think. It contains no condemnation of "media bias." While trotted out routinely to score debate points, this shopworn cliché ultimately does more to stop dialogue than to promote it: specifically, it distracts participants from honestly weighing the validity of the point at hand. Besides, those who condemn the "liberal media" of network news and the *New York Times* should also consider the proliferation of conservative sources like FOX News and talk radio (and vice versa). We'll take another look at this issue when we discuss the "balanced media diet" in chapter 6.

The real threat to dialogue in media, however, lies in the *structure* of media. Consider the trend toward instant access. Newspapers and magazines, with their abundant space for in-depth coverage of issues, are giving way to online media outlets, and the public is following. More people now get their news from the Internet than from traditional news sources, the culmination of a trend that is over ten years old.[5] While the space for reporting online is theoretically unlimited, the instant access encourages shorter attention spans.

The passion for "instant" has taken hold of TV as well. The structure of TV news—so many issues to cover in just thirty or sixty minutes—lends itself to the sound bite and the quick edit, which give the impression that complex issues can be expressed in three seconds or less. Everything on twenty-four-hour news channels seems to be "breaking news," desensitizing us to truly important events happening at the time. Yesterday's catastrophe is easily forgotten in favor of today's dramatic development. When the Bush administration diverted its attention from Afghanistan to Iraq in the years following 9/11, the news media—which, after all, are charged with covering the latest government actions—followed suit, and the military action against al-Qaeda and the Taliban became nearly invisible to the general public.[6] All of these trends, taken together, contribute directly to oversimplification of issues and our cultural ADD.

The rest of television does its share to detract from the cause of dialogue as well. Thirty-second TV commercials are increasingly sharing the airwaves with their ten- and fifteen-second counterparts—another example of the "instant" trend. In an entirely different way, the storytelling motifs of TV dramas serve as a model of counterproductive dialogue. How many times have you watched characters in a romantic relationship talk like this:

ANGELA: It's not that. I just really need you to support me in this one thing.
JOHN: I don't know. I just don't know.
ANGELA: What are you saying? That it's over?
JOHN: No, not that—
ANGELA: Then what?
JOHN: I guess this is it then.
ANGELA: I guess it is.
(cut to new scene)

As a viewer, you wonder, "What on earth just happened?" What just happened is that the characters talked, not with each other or even to each other, but *past* each other. The abrupt scene shift does us no favors, either. How often have you seen characters come to the height of conflict, only to have the scene change? From this we learn (usually destructive) ways to *engage* in conflict, but nothing about *resolving* conflict. With all the television that Americans view—more than 4½ hours per day, according to Nielsen Media Research[7]—it is hard for us *not* to take all this as normal behavior.

And what of reality shows? All too often, they encourage conflict rather than collaboration among contestants; whatever collaboration *does* take place is often tinged with suspicion. Hostility and gossip run through many reality shows as a leitmotif. To be sure, conflict is more interesting than harmony; novelists and playwrights have known this for centuries. But conflict does nothing to foster a climate where dialogue can flourish. Again, by tuning in to these shows, we can easily absorb their subtle lessons as well.

I don't mean any of this as a blanket condemnation of all media. It is not easy to tell a dramatic story in sixty minutes or cover the world's news in thirty. By and large, the people involved in these media are simply trying to fulfill their mission to inform or entertain the public. It is the system itself that, simply by the way it works, detracts from dialogue and makes resolving conflicts that much more difficult.

The Language Shapers

Have you ever checked the news and come across a phrase that made you think, "Where'd *that* come from?" Welcome to the world of the language shapers. With every issue *du jour,* it seems, comes at least one sound bite–friendly word or phrase that subtly shapes public perceptions of the issue. A few examples speak louder than any exposition ever could:

- **"Tax and spend."** When a policy idea involves new expenditures, let alone new or increased taxes, conservatives often trot out this label to condemn it. As a result, the idea's relative merits are lost behind the label. For instance, some commentators have argued for a substantial carbon tax as a way to wean society off dependence on fossil fuels. By making the use of these fuels more expensive, the tax will encourage energy-saving practices and make alternative energies more commercially competitive. All opponents have to do, however, is keep hammering on the word *tax*—with its simplistic subtext that taxes are always bad—to obscure dialogue on the topic.

- **"Micromanaging the war."** When congressional Democrats, fresh from their 2006 election victory, began discussing deadlines for troop withdrawals from Iraq, opponents used this phrase to assert that the military, not the Congress, should direct tactics in wartime. There is something to this assertion, to be sure, and it deserves thoughtful discussion. But does deadline setting really qualify as micromanaging? In my twenty-plus years of running a business, I completed hundreds of projects; nearly every one came with a deadline, a necessary parameter for timely completion. Not once could I have accused a client of "micromanaging" me just because she told me when she wanted the project done.

- **"Pro-choice" or "pro-life"?** Both terms and their associated catchphrases (such as "a woman's right to choose") are effective at succinctly highlighting the main argument behind each position. But neither is entirely accurate, and therefore both terms actually distort the debate while ossifying opinion. Take *pro-choice,* whose connotations ring with the power of individual freedom.

But whose choice? The fetus certainly has none. If there is any chance that the fetus is a human being—a question that, I believe, is fundamentally philosophical or religious and not scientific—the term *pro-choice* mocks its inability to choose life or death for itself. *Pro-life* is no more accurate: to be literally true, it requires a firm stance against capital punishment and most instances of war, but those who are against abortion do not often embrace the other "pro-life" positions.

- **"You animal."** Try this exercise: as you listen to conversation and ingest your daily share of media, count the instances in which people use nonhuman metaphors to refer to anyone who offends them. People on the other side of the political spectrum might become snakes, worms, skunks, weasels, or just plain scum. By labeling them this way, we relieve ourselves of the responsibility of actually weighing their perspectives. After all, why listen to a weasel's opinion on national defense or Federal Reserve policy? Unfortunately, this tactic can morph well beyond name calling into a dangerous trap. At the extreme, consider the number of large-scale inhumanities, including slavery and genocide, that have sprung from one group's regard of another as subhuman.

As with media in general, I am not condemning all shaping of language to make a point. That would defeat a key message of this book, which advocates the use of careful language. The problem arises when people craft their words without regard for the unblinking pursuit of truth—which they do all the time. In my years as an advertising copywriter, I sat through numerous meetings in which someone suggested a catchphrase or slogan for a product, only to have someone else declare it "not exactly true" with a wink and a nudge. The message was clear: the concern for truth was peripheral to the central issue of communicating a point (or it came up only in relation to avoiding a lawsuit). That set of priorities leads us directly to "bending" the truth wherever we can.

So how do these poorly crafted terms detract from dialogue? When we hear them over and over, we begin to assume they are the only way to think about a particular issue. To borrow a business cliché, these terms set the "box"—and make it more difficult to think outside it. Whenever we try to dialogue about these issues, then, we first have to clear away the box and evaluate afresh.

Many language shapers, of course, want us to stay inside the box, because it increases the chances that we will agree with them. Authentic dialogue calls for us to break through.

I'm Really Busy Right Now

Why is everyone so busy? A key contributing factor is the vicious cycle brought on by advances in communication technology. With each leap forward (for example, from overnight delivery to fax to e-mail to text messaging), we delight in our new ability to do things even faster, in more places, than ever before. Then we find we're *expected* to do things faster, in more places, than ever before, because of the very technology we celebrate. Time that we formerly had for reflection—in the car, at home, on vacation—can now be used for work. The culture, in short, speeds up with each new advance.

Few people are objecting with any vigor. By and large, we have bought into the notion that busy is good and busier is better: note the widespread overscheduling of children to provide as many enrichment activities as possible, or the way businesspeople boast about their eighty-hour work-weeks and use the word *busy* as a badge of honor. The press of today's frenetic pace threatens us with the idea that unless we comply, we will neither succeed ourselves nor be able to provide for our loved ones. So we do all we can to keep up, and we never admit to downtime.

Authentic dialogue suffers greatly as a result. By its very nature, dialogue takes time: time to truly hear what the other person says, reflect on it, and engage it with a thoughtful response. My conversation with my sister-in-law Jane (as discussed in the introduction) took place over parts of two days. The breaks gave us time to rest from the intense process of active listening and fully digest what had been said.

Similarly, Quakers have used a method called the Clearness Committee to discern the voice of their "inner teacher" in the face of life transitions and quandaries.[8] A person assembles five or six trusted people to hear her story and ask her honest, open questions, with no hint of leading or giving advice. The goal is to clear away the person's mental clutter and thus allow her to hear the inner voice that will guide her toward a resolution. How long does this take? No less than three hours—plenty of time for the silent reflection that enables the questions to have their full effect. How many people today are willing or able to take part in a three-hour meeting with such a nonmeasurable objective?

On the other side of the attention-span scale, I often found that my clients would ask me a question about a project when I gave them the answer in an e-mail two days before. If people are too busy and distracted to hear one another on relatively simple matters like project details, how can they find the time and attention span to engage in dialogue?

This is why specific strategies in communication and conflict resolution, while very helpful in conducting dialogue, may not be enough to foster a *climate* of dialogue. That requires a change of heart, as we will discuss in the next chapter.

Segregation Lives

While touring San Francisco on foot recently, I hopped a bus that took me from the downtown area up Russian Hill to the wharves. As we passed through a section densely populated with Vietnamese expatriates, I glanced around the bus. There were maybe twenty riders. I was one of only two white Anglo men. And all I could think was, "Cool."

American society is becoming wonderfully diverse. The influx of Latinos/Latinas, Chinese, Indians, and those from many other cultures makes a tremendous impact on the opportunities for dialogue. In essence, it expands our pool of knowledge and perspectives exponentially—giving us even more ways to collaborate, overcome world problems, and build a stronger, more stable society.

That can only happen, however, if we associate with people who are not like us. Alas, all too often we do exactly the opposite, seeking out people with our interests, our perspectives, our worldview, in a de facto segregation. To a large extent, this has always been true, but now it happens virtually as well. In an ironic twist, the very searchability of the Internet—which can connect us with diverse people and ideas more readily than ever before—can also empower us to find, and spend the bulk of our time with, compatible interest groups and like-minded people. This reinforces the way we tend to organize ourselves in neighborhoods, houses of worship, and community groups.

To be sure, people within these groups can disagree on issues, but as we discussed earlier in this chapter, the areas of acceptable disagreement are smaller than with a more diverse group. This reinforces not just our values, but also our language: the catchphrases we use with like-minded people can distract us from considering the deeper thought behind them.

So can the stories. Growing up, I often listened to my parents' friends tell story after disparaging story about "welfare cheats." It was easy to assume from their discussion that *all* people receiving public assistance were cheating. No one was around to suggest that perhaps there was another side to the story.

The Faces of Fear

Most of the obstacles we've discussed are systemic in nature, or at least have a systemic component. Absolute thinkers are trapped in systems of belief; a media system shapes the terms of our dialogue; and so on. Yet this final obstacle is intensely personal.

Ironically, fear is also eminently reasonable. For one thing, when we understand the rigor of dialogue and what it demands of us, *we fear the effort.* This is especially true since some of our most meaningful dialogues carry no immediate benefit and fulfill no urgent objective. Indeed, they may touch on society's largest issues and our deepest feelings about them without any hope of making an impact on these issues.

Perhaps you have enjoyed an honest, respectful discussion with someone, only to have a third person say half-mockingly, "So, have you solved all the world's problems yet?" That response, though usually said in jest, underscores our basic attitude toward dialogue: Why discuss big, ponderous topics when you can't change their course and there are more "important" things to be done here and now? And if authentic dialogue is hard work, isn't that all the more reason to avoid it?

But there are other, deeper fears as well. For instance, *we fear the risk.* We cannot dialogue without exposing our viewpoints, even our most cherished beliefs, to challenge. When people reject our beliefs, we feel they are rejecting us as well. Perhaps even more frightening, we risk discovering the good sense of opposing viewpoints—and even, maybe, the need to adopt them.

During the 1980s, I was passionate in my belief that Ronald Reagan was the personification of everything wrong with the conservative movement. I deplored his administration's military buildup, its interference in Nicaragua's internal affairs, its disregard for the poor, its supply-side economics. Like many others, I laughed at Reagan's Strategic Defense Initiative and called it "Star Wars." The Iran-Contra scandal horrified me.

Over the years, events have confronted me with the need to change my view a bit. One could make the argument that the military buildup accelerated the fall of the Soviet Union, which brought the potential for freedom to millions of people. I have to admit that the tax cuts of Reaganomics benefited people across a wide swath of the economic spectrum, not just the top 10 percent.[9] I still find the Nicaraguan business and the slashing of antipoverty programs loathsome, but my view of Reagan overall is more nuanced.

The point is, I've had to eat crow, and it is a painful experience. Not only do I have to admit I may have been wrong on some things, I risk the scorn of my progressive friends. When we open ourselves to a broader range of opinions—the type of openness that dialogue requires—we also open ourselves to this as well.

Finally, we *fear the anger*. As I alluded to earlier, the deeper the dialogue, the closer it gets to our very essence. It is natural, when we sense this essence being challenged or even attacked, to move into fight-or-flight mode: to either become more strident in our opinions or "be nice" and change the subject. Both prevent us from reaching the benefits that dialogue can bring: authentic harmony with others; openness to diverse insights; a deep, abiding inner peace. The tenor of dialogue we have learned from our society only reinforces our fight-or-flight response. Talk radio and many daytime talk shows have taught us not to channel our feelings into more compelling dialogue, but to devolve into *louder* dialogue.

In short, we either play nice or become vitriolic. Neither response gets us where we want to go.

Again, none of these fears are unreasonable. At least one of them arose from the process of natural selection, and we won't be changing that anytime soon. And yet we must find a way to overcome them. This, I think, is why a reorientation to dialogue as a way of life is so important: this "conversion," as we will see in later chapters, makes us more secure, more confident, more joyful people—far better able to take on the hard work, and reap the profound joy, that dialogue brings.

Where Do We Go from Here?

The polarization of our thinking in the public square. The runaway train that is technological advancement. The all-pervasive media—and the powerful few who would shape it for their own ends.

Yes, the obstacles to dialogue can seem overwhelming. The deck looks stacked against us. Very few of us, if any, are poised to take on such gigantic systems, let alone change them completely.

So we must start with the one thing we *can* change.

FOR YOUR CONSIDERATION ...

1. Consider the obstacles to dialogue presented in this chapter. Which influence you the most? How could you overcome their influence in your own life?

2. How do you use language to support your convictions? What catchphrases are your favorites? How could you reword them to shed more light on your beliefs—and open the door to dialogue?

3. What other obstacles to dialogue come to mind? What kind of influence do they have on you? On the state of dialogue in our society?

4. With what in this chapter do you disagree? Why?

Engaging the Work
of the Soul

Name a figure who single-handedly changed the course of history in the past three hundred years. Without a moment's thought, you might come up with Martin Luther King Jr., or Thomas Jefferson, or Winston Churchill.

And you would be wrong.

The key word here is *single-handedly*. For all of Dr. King's eloquence, courage, and faith, the actions of the civil rights movement—the rallies and the marches and the bus boycotts—would have failed without the millions of people who took part. Despite Jefferson's soaring vision, the United States would still be nothing more than a vision if not for the other Founders, not to mention the thousands of colonists who took up arms. In short, no one changes the world single-handedly. We cannot transform entire social systems with our own two hands.

But we *can* change the fundamental building block of any social system: ourselves.

With the help and grace of God, that change can become something genuine and permanent: a *conversion*. Many of us think of conversion in terms of joining a new denomination or becoming born again. But *conversion* simply means a change of life, a change from the inside out toward a new way of doing things. It is not easy work. Ultimately, however, conversion to the way of dialogue carries benefits that would feed us all: peace of soul, harmony with others, a deeper walk with God, and the power to make the world better than it was before we entered it.

In this conversion process, as in its traditional counterpart, the inner workings of God's grace cultivate virtues and strengths of character in the soul. It is worth a look at five of these virtues, the long-standing misconceptions surrounding them, and what they can mean for us today.

Humility, Not Humiliation

Imagine two cabinetmakers, both of whom excel at their craft. One of them, when praised for his work, demurs with "Oh, they're just cabinets. Nothing special. Anybody could do it." The other cabinetmaker admires the quality of his craftsmanship and the beauty of the cabinets he has made. He counts himself blessed for having such a talent, but he readily admits to it. Which one is the humble cabinetmaker?

Few words generate greater misunderstanding than *humility*. In the minds of many, it has come to signify humiliation or—as displayed by our first cabinetmaker—self-deprecation. Even the dictionary enshrines such definitions. As an adjective (according to *Merriam-Webster's Collegiate Dictionary,* 11th edition), *humble* can mean "ranking low in a hierarchy or scale: insignificant, unpretentious." As a verb, it can signify "to destroy the power, independence, or prestige of." Eating *humble pie* is something no one wants to do. Being *of humble means* is something no one wants to be. In a society like ours, characterized by an aggressive social Darwinism, humility can be the kiss of death.

There is a better way to think about humility, and it can release all kinds of potential within us. Rightly understood, humility is complete clarity about our individual selves and our place in the universe. To quote the associates' rule from one monastic order (Order of the Holy Cross), "Humility is not self-denigration; it is honest appraisal. We have gifts and deficiencies, as does everyone else." This describes our second cabinet-maker to a T. He is the humble one.

When I think about humility in this context, I reduce it to two basic claims:

1. I'm only one person.

2. I *am* one person.

You hear the first claim quite a bit, especially when everyday people talk about social or political issues. "Yeah, the world's a mess, but what can I do? I'm only one person." The truth of this claim is self-evident; a look in the mirror is all the evidence you need.

The fruit of "I'm only one person" is less evident but no less real. First, it is hard to maintain any sense of arrogance—which I define as overestimating your value or capabilities beyond all reality—when you cast a cold eye on your place in the universe. Next time you're in a big city, stop for a moment and watch the throngs of people surging around you. Or, in the woods, gaze at the innumerable stars in the sky on a clear night. Can we really claim that (as many ads would have us believe) we "deserve" a better station in life, a better place in the checkout line, young-looking skin that belies our age? These might be good things, but "I'm only one person" has a way of putting them in a bigger perspective: even, dare we say it, God's perspective.

Second, "I'm only one person" liberates the over-responsible from taking on too much. I know this temptation all too well. If I am not shouldering 90 percent of a group task, I assume I am slacking off. When I first visited the monastery with which I am associated, I made sure the monks knew they could call on me to help around the grounds or clean up after meals. Only recently have I begun to relax in the basic truth of the situation: I am a *guest* at the monastery. The monks do just fine without me. There are, in short, other people to shoulder the load, allowing me to do what I went there for—to listen for God's voice. I'm only one person. I don't *need* to do everything. Once we learn what we can and cannot do, we feel justified in saying no to things that don't fit with our skills, schedule, or purpose, and our lives gain more balance as a result.

Still, taking "I'm only one person" as the *whole* truth can be profoundly corrosive. If you have no power to effect change or create a better world, why bother trying? Why vote, for instance, even in municipal elections, when one vote rarely sways the outcome? No wonder the American voter turnout rate is so low. "I'm only one person," when understood as the whole truth, can lead to despair.

I wonder whether this also affects the type of giving and change making we *do* undertake. Americans in general are well-known for their generosity in times of crisis: we are quick to donate money, food, and other items. Many of us feed the hungry at soup kitchens or build homes for the poor or recycle to preserve the environment. But when an opportunity arises to change the social systems that foster these crises, many of us hold back. Why should I lobby my legislators or write letters to the president or march on Washington? I'm only one person. So if I don't do it, my contribution will not be missed.

It takes the second humility claim to liberate us from this thinking— by giving us the power to do what we can. When you embrace "I *am* one person," you realize that you have exactly one person's gifts, talents, and limitations. (In fact, you may be the *only* person with your set of gifts, talents, and limitations.) You can make exactly one person's contribution to the world. Your potential impact, borne of applying your gifts to the issues that call for them, begins to dawn on you. Once you put those gifts to use in a setting that appreciates them, the validation you receive is empowering indeed: few things feel better than the affirmation of some person, some charity, some house of worship, some soup kitchen that values precisely what you have to offer.

To see how this works, imagine that I want to change my state's law on cell phone use while driving. As "only one person," I look at the power of the legislature, the complexity of the bureaucracy, the staggering challenge of swaying public opinion, and then I look at little old me—and despair. But in "I *am* one person" mode, I look at my gifts and realize I can write. So I write op-ed pieces, letters to the editor, and missives to individual legislators. That is my "one person's contribution."

Are my written arguments enough to change the law? Rarely. And that brings us straight to the next insight: by empowering us individually,

"I *am* one person" opens our eyes to the value of *we*. Once we see both our gifts and our limitations clearly, we begin to grasp that we can accomplish even more, exponentially, by wedding our talents to those of others. The tasks too intimidating for "just one person" suddenly look doable. We begin to band together and do them—creating institutional change, wielding clout with legislators, building coalitions to wield even more clout.

This is where it gets interesting.

To extend our example, I know I can use my writing skills to get the word out about cell phone use. But I cannot spend countless hours lobbying legislators. I know little about recruiting volunteers, and even less about motivating them. Drafting legislation is not in my skill set. In other words, I can't do this by myself. So I try to find groups who are concerned about the law as well. Perhaps in their midst is a community organizer who knows how to rally the troops, and a former congressional aide who could draft bills in her sleep. We put our money together and hire a lobbyist, a measure that my limited income couldn't possibly cover alone. All of a sudden, with all of us doing what we do best, we have impact. Playing to my strengths and limitations has opened my eyes to the power of a group—and my need for such a group to accomplish my goals.

There is another personal benefit to humility understood in this way. Once we discover how we can wield our strengths to greatest effect, we reap the fulfillment that comes from making a serious difference in the world. We become more of the people God intended us to be.

Most important for dialogue, we can see what we know—and how much we don't—by cultivating humility. We can appreciate just how unfathomable the universe, life, and God truly are. From here it becomes clear that the insights and perspectives of others might hold value. Maybe there is value in listening to them after all.

And just like that, we have begun to till the soil of our soul.

Open to the Other

In theory, openness springs directly from humility. As we become more aware of our place in the universe and the limitations of our understanding, as we move naturally from that awareness to consider the insights of others, we become open almost without thinking about it. In theory.

To be sure, this often happens as we cultivate humility in our own souls. But as always, the real world is a bit messier. The deeper we delve into the life of God and the way of dialogue, the more likely we are to find biases of which we were never aware. We get pushed beyond what we consider our limits. Certain bugbears make us think, "Well, yes, I want to be open, but to *that*?"

I wrestle with this quite a bit. My conscious journey with God started in the evangelical world, and those roots have left me with a legacy—some of which I cherish, some of which makes me cringe. The cringe part gets in my way at times. As a result, in my current frame of reference, I am more than ready to listen attentively to Presbyterians, Jews, Muslims, the LGBTQ community,[1] you name it. But *Baptists*? Really?

Really. I can have a crystal-clear understanding of my place in the universe and *still* want to avoid "them" (insert your least favorite group here) like the plague. But the way of dialogue asks us to dialogue with everyone, even—perhaps especially—those who irritate us most. As we happen on those dark prejudices and blind spots in our journey, we may have to make a conscious effort to be still, to listen to the irritating other without reacting: in a word, to cultivate openness.

That cultivation helps us avoid another disconnect between humility and openness as well, one that could easily thwart dialogue before it begins. While grasping our place in the universe, we could simply settle into our own limited, but comfortable, perspectives. I can envision this evolving into a "live and let live" attitude that, while commendable in many respects, doesn't do much for our own spiritual growth or the growth of others. Simply put, it may bring *you* peace, but there's a lot more to the picture than that.

As a Christian, I could recognize the existence of Islam and think to myself, "Muslims think differently, but they're entitled to their beliefs. They can live their way, and I'll live mine." But if that is where I stop, I have not done anything to forge the dialogue that would enable Christians and Muslims to work together in harmony and mutual respect. The titanic challenges of Muslim-Western relations call for us to do more: to move from mere "live and let live" to genuine openness. In answering that call—and cultivating the kindred virtue of openness, intellectual curiosity—we practically drive ourselves into an active exploration of other insights and perspectives. It is one small step from there to honest dialogue with those who hold them dear.

The (Pursuit of) Truth Will Set You Free

Truth has gotten a bad rap for some good reasons. First, some people who stake an exclusive claim to The Truth behave in ways that alienate and wound. Think of Franklin Graham, the son of evangelist Billy Graham, calling Islam "a very evil and wicked religion"[2] or, worse, Osama bin Laden's campaign of terror against anyone he labeled an "infidel." Many people, especially those with no professed faith, extrapolate these extreme actions to *all* quests for truth and reject them as a result. Honestly, it's hard to blame them.

Second, and far more widespread in its influence, is our pervasive relativism. As we discussed in the last chapter, our gloriously diverse society brings us into contact with an equally glorious diversity of viewpoints. Moreover, instant media allow us to see religious and social practices from all over the globe, many of which are completely different from ours. Meanwhile, our secularized culture has granted everyone license to pursue his or her own perspectives; the traditional sources of authority and guidance have lost most of their influence. All these factors, and others like them, combine to leave us with the question: Who are we to judge others' opinions of truth?

The question is not without merit. Holding it in our hearts can lead to tolerance, mutual respect, greater compassion, and, yes, authentic dialogue. I would suggest that in many areas of our lives we should embrace such a viewpoint, at least to the extent that it enables us to listen and enlarge our view of the world.

But adopting it carte blanche presents problems. For one thing, it can devolve into the simplistic "live and let live" approach that we explored in the previous section. Before you know it, we're back to four blind men with their own perspectives, an elephant to move—and no clue as to how to do it.

The other problem with the "There's no right or wrong" approach is that it's, well, wrong. Consider, for example, the sincere Christians of ages past who believed that the Bible gave its stamp of approval to slavery. Today's Christians would call that interpretation wrong. But that opens the door to an unsettling doubt: Are there beliefs or practices today that *we* take for granted but future generations will see as clearly wrong? And if the answer is yes, wouldn't that make the pursuit of truth—no matter how uncomfortable—worthwhile?

Another example: For how many decades did tobacco companies fund research that promoted the safety of smoking? Today, the consensus is that the research was wrong (to say the least); this truth, and the pursuit thereof, saved the lives of millions of smokers who decided to quit as the consensus took shape. The emerging agreement on the truth of climate change may similarly provide the moral force for action.

It is so easy to wreak havoc by labeling beliefs "wrong" that we have to do it with extreme caution. And yet, as the debate over climate change makes clear, the future of our planet may depend on getting many things "right." This makes the pursuit of truth—and the dialogue required to pursue it fully—a necessity.

So, of course, does a belief that is fundamental to our faith as Christians: that God is truth. If we are called to seek God, doesn't it follow that we are also called to seek truth, however elusive it may be in any given instance?

The pursuit of truth, heedless of the consequences, is hardly simple. It can lead us into exploring ideas that are uncomfortable to us. If we find them to be true, we may need to reshape our lives around them, sometimes to the dismay and even hostility of those around us. Think of people whose exploration of truth brought them stiff opposition from the people they loved most. Abolitionists were intimidated and even, in the case of Illinois minister Elijah Parish Lovejoy, murdered for their beliefs.

Not that the pursuit of truth inevitably leads to trouble. Indeed, the whole point of raising this virtue here is its power to bring us together. When we are passionate about truth—not truth as we see it, but truth in itself—we eagerly seek out anyone whose perspective might shed light on that truth. That draws us into an exploration of diverse ideas with other people. In other words, truth seeking as a habit of the heart draws us straight into dialogue.

Facing the Risk

What makes you *you*? How do you define yourself? If you're like many people, descriptors of some sort probably come to mind. You might start with your faith, your career choice, or your station in life: I am a Christian, I am a wife and mother, I am an attorney, I am homeless. Further exploration might bring you into the specifics of your value systems: I am a Democrat, I think *all* life is sacred, I believe people are basically good and fair.

Sometimes these self-definitions are barely conscious. I spent many years refusing to define myself by my work and my income. Only recently have I learned just how deeply I *did* define myself that way—and how profoundly the definition shaped my life.

Whether we acknowledge these definitions or not, we live with them. More than that, they form the infrastructure of our interior life. We draw on them to sustain ourselves and make sense of the world. As we age and accumulate more life experience, this infrastructure becomes more highly developed—and, frequently, less flexible. Hence the comment often heard about people of a certain age: "They're so set in their ways."

Now throw authentic dialogue into the mix.

Once we open ourselves to the perspectives of others, anything can happen, as we saw in the previous chapter. Elements of our belief systems come up against realities they do not explain. We may even discover that we have been completely wrong in certain areas. It is a profoundly disorienting experience. No wonder we are often so unwilling to risk serious dialogue.

And yet willingness to risk is an essential character trait in fostering that dialogue. So how do we overcome our resistance? By seeing ourselves in an entirely new light: by answering the question "What makes you *you*?" more deeply, in a way that frees us to hold our opinions more lightly. When we do that, we can look at our infrastructure afresh. We suddenly have the freedom and inner resources to say, "But I could be wrong," which is essential to authentic dialogue.

Circumstances can push us toward that point. A devout, newly married couple wants to start a family. They believe that one parent should stay home with the children—even that God's will requires it—but they can barely scrape by on one income as it is. Clearly something has to give. They could postpone children until they are more financially secure. One of them could seek a higher-paying job or move into a new career. Maybe, though, they reexamine their belief about one parent staying home with the children, discovering not that God requires it, but that their own experience of two working parents left them feeling abandoned during their growing-up years. They no longer have to define themselves by this belief, and they are thus free to uphold, adapt, or reject it. More to the point, they can now enter the dialogue about starting a family with a clearer sense of themselves, the place of their values in their life together, and how flexible they could be.

Ultimately, to be most effective, this process of preparing ourselves for risk involves getting in touch with what truly *does* define us: our soul as it lives in God. The clearest path to that redefinition is a deeper connection with God, as we will discuss later in this chapter.

If I Have Not Love, I Can Do Nothing

The redefinition of ourselves may well be the first step toward acquiring the most important virtue of all: a commitment to love. Once we separate our myriad perspectives and positions from our own essential identity as image bearers of God, we can do the same with others. We begin to see them for who they are: not their perspectives or opinions, but their *selves*. That allows us to care for them as people—to take their inner conflicts and concerns to heart—no matter how vehemently we disagree with them. Compassion naturally flows from this new perspective. When we strip away all the externals, we see the image of God in each person.

Sometimes this new view of someone happens all by itself. See if this sounds familiar: You're talking with an adversary, teeth clenched, when suddenly she reveals a completely different side of herself. You discover she's been struggling with depression for twenty years, or her parents are dying, or she volunteers at a homeless shelter in her spare time. In situations like that, we often say we've "seen the human side" of the other person. More accurately, we see that the sum total of the other person far transcends the things that drive us crazy. Our reaction to such moments is almost automatic: sympathy, an ebbing of our anger, a softening of heart.

Now this may sound like a one-time breakthrough, after which you and your adversary live happily ever after. Alas, it is not, any more than love is a one-time act. Because our relationships endure, day after day after day, we are faced with the challenge of loving day after day after day. The things that irritate us about the other person naturally crowd back into our consciousness as we encounter them, and they often overwhelm our vision of God's image within. Just because I adore my wife for who she is—for the qualities that make up her very essence—doesn't mean I remain calm when she leaves our back door wide open in midwinter five days in a row. This is where the commitment comes in: the pledge that I *will* be there for her, that I will set myself aside and do whatever I can to foster the unfolding of her best self, no matter what.

This commitment has everything to do with dialogue. Indeed, it liberates us to *have* dialogue. If we are committed to each other, we suddenly can disagree, even vehemently, without fear of severing the relationship. Even more important, we go into the very act of dialogue with the other's benefit foremost in mind.

Can dialogue damage this commitment by descending into vitriol? Absolutely, if our passion for a particular position or value gets the better of us. But part of the commitment to love is a commitment to prevent that from happening. It is far more difficult to go for the throat when your framework is to cherish the other's interest as well as—or more than—your own.

Perhaps Thomas Aquinas summed up the call to love and dialogue most succinctly. "We must love them both, those whose opinions we share and those whose opinions we reject," he wrote. "For both have labored in the search for truth and both have helped us to find it."

To Turn, Turn

How do we get there from here? How do we till our soul so that these virtues grow and flourish?

Certainly practice plays an important role. The longer we practice these virtues, the more they become woven into our own selves; we see ever more clearly the value of others, the merit of their opinions, the importance of truth, and our place in the universe—all the essentials for engaging others in authentic dialogue.

For two reasons, however, practice alone is often insufficient to effect lasting change. One is the typical failure of sheer grit and determination, of "trying hard to be better." By itself, force of will may work sporadically or for the short term. Ultimately, however, it is like dieting: how many people can lose weight—and keep it off—just by trying hard? It is simply too easy to go back to the banana muffins and the candy and the tortilla chips after we reach our goal weight, especially when we get too busy or overwhelmed to pay rigorous attention to what we are eating. In the same way, it is simply too easy to fall back into old patterns when we do not have the time or energy to practice the virtues.

The other reason that practice is not sufficient, though, involves the position in which progress toward these virtues puts us. By practicing humility, by opening ourselves to the insights of others, by seeking truth regardless of our own beliefs, we make ourselves extraordinarily vulnerable—especially to those who, shaped by the prevailing culture, continue to attack us and defend themselves. The willingness to risk is one thing; the emotional capacity to risk is quite another. It calls for an inner strength that few of us can muster alone.

This is where conversion comes in.

Like its antiquated counterparts, the word *conversion* means something a bit different in today's religious climate. Many people use it to describe the born-again experience: a one-time receiving of Christ into one's heart. That is a critical part of the conversion experience, and it forms the foundation of our ability to dialogue. When we enter into this relationship with God, we no longer need to muster the inner strength alone—because we no longer *are* alone.

There is another aspect to the word *conversion,* though, that this use doesn't quite capture: its status as a lifelong process. Benedictines express this fuller meaning in the phrase *conversion of life.* Understood in this way, conversion implies a slow, persistent turning of one's life, from the inside out, to something different, something better. The Shakers capture this process in their magnificent hymn:

To turn,
Turn will be our delight,
Till by turning,
Turning we come round right.

But how exactly does conversion lead to the virtues necessary for dialogue? To answer that, first consider the profound connection of these virtues—particularly humility, love, and truth—to the very heart of God. As the prophet Micah says, "What does the Lord require of you but to do justice, and to love kindness, and to walk humbly with your God?" (Micah 6:8). When we foster our own personal connection with God, then, we gradually begin to reflect these dialogue-enhancing virtues as we reflect God's image. *This* is conversion.

And this is why people of faith are uniquely positioned to lead the effort toward dialogue: because they already know the One who supports and converts from within. Anyone with a heart for God can foster this relationship and the virtues that go with it.

But how?

Face-to-Face with the Divine

Books about the encounter with God could fill several libraries,[3] so an exhaustive study of spiritual practices is well beyond our scope here. However, I can share what I know from the Christian tradition. And what I know comes in four forms that you may find useful, too.

First and foremost is the practice of *silent prayer*. Many people, even longtime believers, think of prayer exclusively as talking *to* God. While this is an essential element of prayer—"Pour out your heart before Him" (Psalm 62:8), the psalmist writes—it is not the only element. By sitting in silence, focusing our attention on the present moment and the Spirit within it, we provide space for God to speak gently to, and move within, our souls. Our sense of this Presence can be exhilarating and centering, which makes us yearn to seek it more and more. As we then make silence part of our regular spiritual practice, God uses it to transform us from the inside out.

There are many practices to facilitate the process. Some people designate a place in their home specifically for prayer: it can include traditional elements of worship, like a cross, candles, and incense, or it can simply be the little-used desk in the corner of the living room where you meet God. The practice of centering prayer—of sitting silently and focusing on a single word, like *Jesus* or *love*—has proved fruitful for millions of people. I find that it enables God to enter my consciousness almost through the back door, as it were; God is there before I know it.[4] Focused attention on an icon similarly provides a window on this encounter—a "thin place," as the Celts would have called it.

The practice of silent prayer does not have to involve ornate visuals and formal practices, however. One gentleman in France was reported to visit a Catholic church every day, sit in one of the pews, and simply gaze at the crucifix; when asked what he was doing, he replied, "I look at him, he looks at me, and we're happy together."[5] It can be that simple. The key is to be silent, wait, receive.

If this is *all* we did, however, our experience of God would be limited to our own experience—and God is just too big for one person alone to grasp. This is why several other traditions are essential to our spiritual formation as people open to dialogue.

Take the *praying of the scriptures.* The Church's great source for this type of prayer has always been the psalms, partly because the psalms convey a vast range of human emotion as expressed to God. The typical monastic practice is to gather in community several times a day to chant the psalms, together with scripture readings and other prayers, a practice commonly known as the Daily Office or Divine Office. There is a beauty and a power to the Office, chanted communally, that is worth experiencing. On the other hand, I only have the time to do this once a day, silently, in the morning, over breakfast. That works, too. Whatever fits your schedule, consistency is the key: praying the Office regularly—especially on those days when we're distracted or just don't feel like it—gets us out of ourselves, a key both to dialogue and to the Christian life itself.

Similarly, it is helpful to pray all the psalms according to a regular cycle, such as the lectionary found in many churches. By doing this, we avoid the temptation to pray only the texts we like. Conversely, we often find ourselves praying texts that *don't* express what we're feeling on a particular day.

This clash between ourselves and another frame of mind brings all sorts of things to light: new ways to think about God, disturbing possibilities that God is not *exactly* the way we understand God, reminders that we are not the center of the universe. By allowing the deepest part of ourselves to encounter wisdom outside ourselves—day after day after day—we not only become larger of spirit, but also gain the perspective on ourselves and the cosmos that authentic dialogue requires.

The same is essentially true of the *study of the scriptures*. The Bible is so utterly unlike us on so many levels. Its books were written in a radically different time and social context; its messages run counter to our society's norms; it includes literary forms, hyperbole, and symbolism that we find difficult to grasp; its ancient assumptions about life may appear nonsensical to us. As a result, any purposeful encounter with the Bible, in any format, will confront us with something very different from ourselves. *Lectio divina*—the slow, contemplative reading of scripture to hear God's voice—may bring this disparity home with the greatest impact, as it engages mind, heart, *and* spirit in an encounter with the Holy.[6]

As with praying the psalms, adherence to a lectionary forces us to grapple with a broader range of the biblical texts. It is not easy to read about God's judgment on a day when God's mercy would feel so much better, or to encounter "My yoke is easy and my burden is light" when life feels anything but. That, to some extent, is the point: to ensure that our view of God—and of the world—is not too small or simplistic.

So these encounters with the scriptures can broaden our perspective. Even so, it is possible to read Genesis to Revelation and still live inside our own heads, because we draw only from our own encounters. Hence the *practice of community*. In the interchange with a group of people, we are confronted with worldviews and frames of reference that we never could have imagined ourselves. We find entirely new ways of viewing old truths. We open up still further to the possibilities of truth and the value of "I could be wrong." If this sounds familiar, it should: in this regard, the fruits of community are the fruits of dialogue itself.

By the time I joined my Episcopal parish, I had already spent a couple of decades studying and exploring my faith. In the years since, however, the good people of the parish have introduced me to approaches that never would have crossed my mind. I knew, for instance, that I took the Bible seriously but not literally, yet only through my membership did I learn about the role of historical and literary criticism in approaching the scriptures. I talked with people who deny a literal resurrection of Jesus and those who would have been quite comfortable in the Church of the Middle Ages. Some of these encounters upset my theological applecart from time to time, and I did not feel a need to accept any of the approaches wholesale. Ultimately, though, they have led me to a richer, more complex understanding of my faith—and a respect for an even broader range of opinions.

Of course, any group of people could work in this way. Community, however—the dedication to a specific group of people, come what may— provides a safe place for the virtues to blossom in our soul. By nurturing that safety, we facilitate the willingness to risk. By persisting with people we may not even like, so as to cultivate their growth and our own, we foster our ability to love. By conflicting with others, then working out our differences, we come to see ourselves as one person in a group, and so we grow in humility. At the most basic level, our living in community is simply our commitment to love fleshed out in a specific time and place.

Our society does not do community well. American history, in particular, has unfolded in such a way that the primacy of the individual is a natural result. The loosening of social constraints over the past fifty years has reinforced this focus on the self. Not that this is entirely bad: it has brought a greater sensitivity to the unique makeup of each individual and fostered a proliferation of choices for people to find their own paths.

But when we "do our own thing" to the exclusion of others, we do so at our collective peril. The blind men can tell us all about that.

Turning Outward

The work of the soul is often portrayed as a solitary, interior practice ("navel gazing," the skeptics would say). And indeed, a great deal of this work finds its center in an inner space where we reflect and pray and contemplate. Yet, paradoxically, these virtues and practices also foster a fundamental crosscurrent in the soul: a broadening to the outside world. When we study sacred texts receptively, we open ourselves to the outside world. When we cultivate humility, we admit that we *must* open our-selves to the outside world or our growth will be stunted and our lives limited. When we engage in community and commit ourselves to love, we immerse ourselves in the outside world.

While the work of the soul opens us to that world, other practices engage it directly. By doing so, they, too, prepare us for dialogue in their own unique way.

FOR YOUR CONSIDERATION ...

1. What are your most cherished beliefs? Why do you cherish them?

2. What do you consider the greatest threat to these beliefs? How could you (if at all) see that threat as simply another perspective? Is it appropriate to do so?

3. Try one of the spiritual disciplines listed in this chapter for a week—or, even better, a month. (See the appendix for basic how-tos.) How does it affect you? What insights have you gathered? Do you see any difference in yourself or the way you see the world?

4. Do you belong to a faith community? If so, how do the beliefs of the community support—or challenge—your own beliefs? How (if at all) does it nurture the virtues of dialogue in your soul? If not, where *do* you seek out the benefits of community for your own life? How does it help you to grow?

5. With what in this chapter do you disagree? Why?

Three Mind-Sets
for the Journey

A few years back, my family ran headlong into a period of extreme stress. One of our loved ones was suddenly beset with dire health issues, and we were on tenterhooks for about two years: planning endless doctor visits, watching for the next symptom, wondering how on earth we were going to make it through.

In the midst of it all, my right thumb stopped bending.

I am double-jointed in my thumbs, so to lose range of motion in that particular digit was strange and a bit unnerving. Every now and then I'd try flexing it to confirm that I hadn't imagined the whole thing. Sure, stress can do peculiar things, but a *thumb*?

Eventually, thank God, our loved one recovered. The family moved into a happier place. And my thumb regained its normal function.

If you have ever had a stress headache, or watched someone's personality change after weeks of chronic pain, or felt your mood elevate as you spent time in sunlight, you know the experience—and, probably, the point I'm about to make. One of the big leaps forward in postmodern thinking is our tendency to view ourselves as a unified whole: a seamless flow of body, mind, and spirit. As a civilization, we are beginning to understand how emotional stress impacts physical ailments. Research has clarified how diet and exercise affect mood. Meditation, considered an "Eastern practice" only a few decades ago, is now recommended to relieve anxiety. The stigma of mental illness is starting to recede (though it still has miles to go) as the understanding of it as a medical issue grows. Mind affects body; body affects spirit; spirit affects body; body affects mind.

So it is with dialogue as a habit of the heart. The work of the soul, as described in chapter 4, generates new mind-sets to take with us into dialogue. Our "heart for dialogue" and these mind-sets inspire us to new actions, new behaviors, new ways of living, that in turn reinforce the changes in our inner lives.

While all these components connect seamlessly, exploring them individually helps our left brain get hold of the concepts. Later, in chapter 6, we'll examine some of the actions we can take to reinforce our inner work. For now, let's look at the mind-sets—our worldviews, our ways of approaching the reality around us—and examine three phrases that can bend them toward dialogue.

The Power of Our Words

"Sticks and stones may break my bones, but names can never hurt me."

My mother would use this old saw to comfort and encourage me when the taunts of the neighborhood kids drove me to tears. As you can imagine, it didn't work. It's a relic from a time when we did *not* see ourselves as whole beings, when the only type of "real" injury was physical injury.

We know better now. The groundswell to prevent bullying is ample (and welcome) evidence of that. So is the stigma that now surrounds the use of racial epithets, ethnic jokes, and stereotypes. Moreover, the impact of our words is hardly limited to other people. When we use words that wound (or heal), we wound (or heal) ourselves in the process. Our words not only affect others, but permeate our own attitudes.

This is hardly a new insight. The apostle James excoriated the power of destructive words in his biblical letter: "The tongue is a fire. The tongue is placed among our members as a world of iniquity; it stains the whole body, sets on fire the cycle of nature, and is itself set on fire by hell.... No one can tame the tongue—a restless evil, full of deadly poison" (James 3:6, 3:8).

So words can affect our mind-sets. Not surprisingly, they also shape the habits of the heart. This is one reason for praying the psalms, as described in chapter 4: as we pray them every day over years, the familiar phrases form the framework of our conception of God. When I regularly encounter "The Lord is king; let the peoples tremble!" (Psalm 99:1) and "The Lord is my shepherd, I shall not want" (Psalm 23:1) together with "God's steadfast love endures forever" (Psalm 136:1) and "Your wrath lies heavy upon me" (Psalm 88:7) as well as "The Lord laughs at the wicked, for God sees that their day is coming" (Psalm 37:13), the boundless complexity of God confronts me again and again and again. My conception of God becomes far more nuanced and multi-dimensional, and so, as a result, does my relationship with God. In the process, I believe, it makes the relationship more enduring—better able to weather the storms of life.

Could other words do the same for dialogue as a habit of the heart? Are there words and phrases that go beyond describing dialogic *practice* and make us—at our core—more dialogic *people?*

In my own pursuit of dialogue, three phrases have emerged to change my orientation toward others. Their frequent use—in my thinking, my speech, and my writing—has contributed to making me more open to dialogue from the inside out.

I Don't Know

Some years ago, I made the acquaintance of a deeply traditional priest. (We will get to know him better in chapter 8.) He bemoaned the lack of teaching authority in Christendom and even looked longingly back to the Church of the Middle Ages. Yet, as we discussed the creeds of the Church and the certainty of some believers, he said, "Remember, even the creeds don't start with *I know,* but *I believe.*"

A pearl of wisdom indeed, and it applies almost everywhere you look. Scientific researchers continually remind us about how much we don't know, whether the topic is dark energy, subatomic particles, the health effects of artificial sweeteners, or the migration of birds. Our global economic uncertainty has exposed the limits of our collective ability to predict what will happen if governments reduce their fiscal deficits to 3 percent of GDP or raise taxes on the top-earning 1 percent or change interest rates. Historians uncover new evidence to refute long-held assumptions about historical "facts."

This goes double for our knowledge about God. Yes, we have marvelous resources at our disposal to help us grapple with God: scripture, the tradition and teaching of the Church, the indwelling Spirit, our own experience. Together they can foster a knowledge of, and connection to, God that is solid enough to provide direction for our lives.

But certainty, I have come to believe, is a chimera. Scripture has gone through myriad cycles of translation and interpretation. Its pages confront us with points and counterpoints, passages that seem at stark variance with each other. To take just a few examples: If God is love, how do we explain the driving out of indigenous peoples described in the book of Joshua—a campaign that, according to the text, took place at God's command? Can God be both the God of Hosea (Hosea 11:8–9), who refuses to give up on the wayward people of Israel, and the "jealous God" of Exodus, ready to destroy them at the first instance of idolatry? What are we to make of Moses's arguments *against* that destruction, which actually change God's mind (Exodus 32:1–14)?

This is difficult terrain, as we all know. Christians have debated how to read the Bible for centuries. Theologians and everyday believers on *all* sides have developed coherent narratives to answer the questions above and others like them. These narratives may well be correct; they do hold wisdom. In any event, Christians throughout history have found enough truth about God in the pages of scripture to love God and live faithfully. But certainty is asking too much.

The same goes for our other sources of knowledge. Hearing the voice of God often takes months, even years, of careful discernment and consulting with others. At bottom, though, it is something we hear within ourselves, where the constructs of certainty cannot reach. The tradition of the Church, like the scripture, has evolved over time in many ways and is itself subject to interpretation. A rigid adherence to it would prevent us (as it did the religious leaders in the Gospels) from noticing when God revealed the Divine Self in new ways.

So there's a lot we don't know, and little if any ground for certainty. In one way, however, all this is beside the point—because certainty is over-rated anyway. The quest for certain knowledge obscures the inestimable value of *I don't know*.

To get a glimpse of that value, it would help to look at wisdom from another faith tradition. Gil Fronsdal, a Buddhist teacher, suggests a meditation practice that involves adding *I don't know* to every thought. In meditation and throughout our daily lives—especially when we find ourselves judging our actions or those of others—we would respond with *I don't know*.

"Repeating the words 'I don't know' allows us to question tightly held ideas," Fronsdal writes. "Done thoroughly, 'I don't know' can pull the rug out from under our most cherished beliefs."[1]

As Christians, by definition, we are not as oriented toward wholesale rug pulling as our Zen colleagues are. We do hold and cherish certain beliefs as hallmarks of our faith tradition. Nonetheless, Fronsdal's observation highlights how *I don't know* opens us to a wealth of virtues that orient us toward dialogue—including some of the character strengths we discussed in chapter 4. For one thing, we become more *curious*. If I truly don't know what I thought I knew, how can I find out more? Do some of my cherished beliefs need adjusting in the face of new information or insight? Could other worldviews hold different yet valuable insights that my worldview doesn't encompass? This newfound curiosity drives us to learn about those worldviews.

It also leads us to *humility*. As we discussed in chapter 4, humility calls us to see ourselves as one person among billions, with one perspective among billions, and the questions we ask out of our curiosity reinforce that view. The more curious we are, the more we admit that we don't know, the more clarity we gain about our place in the universe, and the more we redouble our efforts to seek out other perspectives.

It is one small step from there to a third virtue of *I don't know: interconnection.* When I begin to explore other ideas, I become more curious about *your* ideas—and about you. I wonder how you and I can complement each other's strengths, limitations, and perspectives. Clearly there is value in listening to you. Unleash this dynamic in a group, and you have the beginnings of a network, if not a community.

This, I think, is the ultimate value of *I don't know* as a mind-set. By recognizing our limitations, exploring other perspectives, and identifying one another as the source of those perspectives, we begin to see one another as valued people, as valued sources of wisdom. We start to treat one another with respect, honor, even love—and reach out to one another in dialogue.

And Yet

"The Iraq war was a terrible idea based on faulty intelligence" … and yet it improved the lot of many Iraqis. "Tea Partiers are uneducated and shallow of thought" … and yet their percentage of college graduates is half again above the national average.[2] "Same-sex marriage will hurt and confuse children" … and yet a longitudinal study reveals that the children of lesbian parents are doing better than their counterparts in other family structures.[3]

The beauty of *and yet* is that it stops us dead in our tracks. We think we have an issue figured out, which entitles us to dismiss—or, worse, disdain—those who disagree. *And yet* as a mind-set opens the way for a new perspective, new evidence, or new thinking to confront us, to turn our minds a little, when we have, even temporarily, made up our minds.

From there the possibilities multiply. Maybe we maintain our own beliefs but have to qualify them in the face of this new idea. Maybe the position of the "other side" has some valid points after all. It *might* even be more valid than our own.

Like *I don't know, and yet* both springs from and reinforces the virtue of humility. Aware of our status as one person among billions, we find it much easier to embrace those *and yet* moments, to consider the other side with openness and curiosity. Conversely, the more we practice *and yet* as a mind-set, the more we become aware of ourselves as *not* the sole arbiter of truth, and the deeper that humility roots itself in our hearts.

By stopping us in our tracks, *and yet* also blocks us from rushing to judgment—a plague endemic to our age. The always-on nature of cable and Internet news media, with their competitive need to broadcast "breaking news" first, has created a tidal wave of information, pushing us to process, analyze, and form opinions with ever-increasing speed. The hectic pace at which many of us live our lives exacerbates this. Based on hastily gathered (and, as a result, often simplistic) scraps of information, the resulting snap judgments leave no room for nuance. *And yet* reopens that room, even for an instant, forcing us to look more deeply into the complexity that nearly every issue carries.

Where does this lead us? To a place similar to where we find ourselves when we adopt *I don't know*. As *and yet* nudges us to consider alternative viewpoints and nuances, it also awakens us to the reasonableness of the people raising them. Our respect for them grows naturally. The next time we encounter them, whether on this issue or another, we are more likely to hear them, and (assuming we continue to find them reasonable) our respect grows even more in a virtuous cycle. With that respect comes a willingness, even an eagerness, to dialogue.

We can, of course, simply allow our interactions with others to shape our thinking in this way. The advantage of adopting *and yet* as an a priori mind-set, however, is that it reshapes our mental framework toward open-mindedness long before the interaction ever takes place. As a result, we approach others with openness—and therefore orient ourselves toward dialogue—right from the start.

Both/And

Either/or has come to dominate the American public square. Elected officials and political parties believe they get more mileage from casting complex issues as *either/ors*. News media, with their limited time for coverage and their competitive pressures, often reinforce simplistic caricatures of these issues. Rather than weigh the merits of banking regulation or reflect on the efficacy of fiscal stimulus, we're told that we either believe in individual freedom or prefer a government takeover of everything. We are either Republican wingnuts or rabid socialists. Ad nauseam.

The problems with this approach are legion, and at least one of them blocks our way to dialogue. *Either/or,* in short, severely narrows the range of possible solutions while making it easy to demonize those on the "wrong" side of this false divide. When there are only two positions in a debate and the issue is drawn in black and white, the people on the other side appear for all the world to be wrong, if not duplicitous or even sinister.

We saw this unfold during the recent installment of our grand national debate over health care. When the discussion heated up in 2009, a whole spectrum of interesting ideas popped up. The more I read and listened, the more I believed that nearly *every* idea had merit, from both sides of the aisle: the public option, the insurance exchange, competition among insurers across state borders, and others. The chances for honest, serious public discourse seemed promising indeed. Yet, as the legislation drew closer to final passage, we heard precious little beyond public-option-versus-no-public-option, "government takeover of health care" versus "the party of no." *Either/or.*

Catholic theologians have long promoted the antidote for *either/or.* *Both/and* enables them to hold the "opposite" sides of many doctrinal issues in a harmonious tension: Jesus as both human and divine, God as both one and three, the Bible as both the Word of God and the product of human writers. Contrary to *either/or, both/and* provides room to embrace divergent views from a broad range of people.

The BothAnd Project—a collaboration between the Mainstream Media Project and the Harvard Global Negotiation Project that aimed to introduce new forms of constructive interaction into the broadcast media—explained *both/and* well on its website. "Instead of assuming that *either* one side *or* the other is correct, BothAnd maintains that *both* one side *and* the other (or others) hold pieces of the answer and that only by combining the best of each can we invent the hybrid solutions that enable us to attain our highest rather than lowest common denominator."[4]

Both/and, granted, has its pitfalls. It is not hard to imagine *both/and* as a mask for lazy thinking, a way to avoid making difficult but important distinctions, or a simplistic rush to "Let's all just get along." Rightly used, though, *both/and* can move us toward genuine syntheses and grand ideas that are far more than the sum of their parts. The trick is to use *both/and* not as a goal, but as a starting point, asking, "*How* can *both/and* work here?" This leads us into a search for new or undiscovered ways in which two "opposing" ideas can combine to create a better one. We consider the merits of various hybrids. We observe the subtleties of each idea and how they work. As part of the process, we learn more about the ideas at hand and open ourselves to reevaluating them at every turn.

Like its counterparts *I don't know* and *and yet, both/and* opens us to inclusion. In *both/and,* we broaden the range of ideas we will entertain. As we include those ideas in our thinking, we include the people who hold them dear. Our circle of welcome, and of dialogue, grows.

Keeping It Real

Our skeptical age gives voice to many misconceptions about the life of the spirit (and the mind). Perhaps the most corrosive is that spirituality is antithetical to the "real world." In this view, mysticism is navel gazing, and therapy simply psychobabble. Ultimately, what matters is what people do, how they act.

In a way, this skepticism runs counter to the emphasis on human wholeness that we discussed at the beginning of this chapter: if we are spirit, mind, and body, it would follow that all three are essential to our fruitfulness on this earth. On the question of action, however, skeptics and mystics actually agree. St. Teresa of Avila, the great Spanish mystic of the sixteenth century, may have had elaborate visions and spectacular encounters with God—but she insisted in *The Interior Castle* (VII, iv, 6) that the point of pursuing the "spiritual marriage" between self and God is "finding ways to please Him," that from the spiritual marriage "are born good works and good works alone." In his parable of the sheep and the goats (Matthew 25:31–46), the Jesus of the Gospels dramatically illustrates that what people do, the compassion they act out, is an essential part of their membership in the kingdom of God.

Indeed, despite what the skeptics would have you believe, the life of the spirit and the mind is remarkably practical. Many of its practitioners undergo inner transformation at least in part to make a difference in the world. Everything in this book up to now, then, has been more "real world" than our age often admits.

In their practicality, then, our discussions to this point flow seamlessly into the "real world" side of dialogue—the steps we can take in the world around us to reorient our lives even more thoroughly. It is to those steps that we now turn.

FOR YOUR CONSIDERATION ...

1. Think of a time when you suddenly saw the merit of someone else's argument or belief. How did you feel? How did you react? What happened to the conversation? What lessons can you take from that experience into the rest of your life?

2. Various words, phrases, or observations strike different people in different ways. How do the three phrases in this chapter strike you? What other phrases or mind-sets might help you become more oriented toward dialogue?

3. With what in this chapter do you disagree? Why?

Pushing beyond Our Borders

Everyone attends the College of Hard Knocks sooner or later. But what if you earned your PhD there?

Think of the way this college works. We leave our childhoods behind and somehow, through trial and painful error, learn to buy car insurance, do our jobs, paint a room, pick a school system for our children, age, grieve. When we face catastrophic circumstances, we strive to derive lessons from them. Every hard-knocks encounter with the world hones our view of the world in some way, large or small, and leaves us with still more questions to ponder. At the same time, it gives us more material to bring to the dialogue table. This is everything a curriculum in the real world should be.

Now consider what the doctoral program looks like. The more encounters we have, the broader our perspective becomes; the broader our perspective, the more we appreciate how little we know, and the better equipped we are for dialogue. How much better equipped would we be, then, if we moved far beyond our usual experiences to get up-close glimpses of the rest of the world?

As we discussed at the end of chapter 4, the work of the soul nudges us in that direction—but we can take the initiative as well. There are many ways to encounter the world beyond us; in this chapter we'll look at three that I've found particularly useful.

The Balanced Media Diet

We love to complain about the media. If there is one issue on which conservatives and liberals can join hands and agree, it's condemnation of media bias. (Never mind that each person has different media in mind when decrying said bias.) In the midst of any good media-trashing session, however, one obvious truth gets lost: of *course* the media are biased. They're made up of people—all of them shaped by their own upbringings, experiences, and values.

(Not that everything we read is deliberately colored to serve a particular agenda, as some pundits would have us think. I believe that most journalists do their level best to present a thorough, balanced picture of their subject, or to bring underreported aspects of a story to light. Editors often give a certain slant to their editorial pages, true, but the best ones aim to include at least some views from across the spectrum. Perfect objectivity, however, is beyond the realm of human possibility.)

As a result, no one media outlet can ever provide the breadth of perspective we need for thoughtful dialogue. Our goal, then, is to ingest a "balanced media diet": a healthful blend of newspapers, magazines, websites, blogs, television news, and other sources that provide a cross-section of viewpoints. In other words, sticking exclusively to the *National Review,* FOX News, *Mother Jones,* or the Huffington Post won't prepare you for dialogue; taking in all four just might. (It might also make you the most interesting person at any cocktail party.)

To be most effective, this cross-section should cover more than just the "conservative-liberal" spectrum. What if we balanced, say, free-market publications with those whose slant is more toward government oversight? What if we mixed in media targeted to racial, gender, or ethnic groups other than our own? Or perused magazines for atheists as well as believers? Perhaps we should include media that themselves present an extensive diversity of opinions. Think of these media as the "mutual funds" of news and opinion. Because each mutual fund is, all by itself, a diverse array of investments, so investing in several mutual funds exposes you to an exceptionally broad range of the financial markets. In the same way, taking in these diverse media might well serve to maximize the breadth of our perspective per hour spent ingesting the news.

In my own life, I seem to have gravitated toward this sort of "mutual fund" news. From *The PBS NewsHour* I get in-depth investigations of a few issues each evening, usually with a well-struck balance of insight and opinion. Our local newspaper carries a diverse blend of columns by conservatives, liberals, and everyone in between, from (to name two of my favorite columnists) David Brooks to Thomas Friedman. In the pages of *Tikkun* I read social and spiritual insights from across the spectrum of faith traditions. Because of its thoughtful insights and analysis, *The Economist* also makes my list; it gives me an ardent bias toward the free market while covering some of the world's least reported stories.

What happens when we take in a diverse media mix, whether "mutual fund" or not? Inevitably, we come across the same story from different angles—and begin to see the legitimacy of each point of view. The complexity of the situation and the lack of easy answers become clear. Almost automatically, we approach the whole issue with a little more humility, a little more openness to others whose viewpoints are different from our own.

Just as important, we grow instinctively skeptical of easy answers for *any* issue, because so few of them work. We start to see slogans and catchphrases as the empty bromides they usually are. "Drill, baby, drill," the energy-policy mantra of the 2008 Republican national convention, doesn't seem so convincing when you've read about estimates of remaining oil reserves and the time frame required to ramp up production, not to mention the environmental risks.[1] "Tax the rich" sounds like a wonderful solution to budget deficits until you've seen estimates of the impact such a policy would have—and how large a deficit would remain.[2]

We even start to take political and social heroes with several grains of salt, knowing how fallible humans are and how quickly we fall. As a New Yorker, I should have known better than to be bedazzled by Eliot Spitzer, the now-disgraced former governor, but a longing for reform in state government overcame my good sense. That experience, however, prepared me for the 2008 presidential campaign: I found myself enthusiastic about Barack Obama but more careful, appreciating his call to come together but always on the lookout for potential faults. As part of that lookout, I searched my balanced media diet to get a more nuanced—and more realistic—picture of the man.

Does this mean we should read everything we can put our hands on? I think the bias is in that direction, but it comes with several caveats. One, clearly, is time: none of us can read more than a tiny segment of the news and opinion published daily. On another point, breadth isn't everything. While pursuing a diversity of media to expand our perspectives, we can easily miss out on the *depth* required as well. Pursuing depth opens us even more to dialogue because, for many issues, the deeper we dive, the more elusive the "right answer" becomes. It is tempting for us to read the weekly newsmagazines (conservative and liberal), start seeing the same basic facts about the Israeli-Palestinian conflict, and conclude that we have something of a handle on the situation. How much better informed we would be, and how much greater our understanding of all sides would be, were we to pore over a thirty-thousand-word article on the long history of Jerusalem. Suddenly we would appreciate the depth of reverence the city inspires, not in one faith tradition, but in three; one "side" could not be granted control over Jerusalem without harming the others.

A diverse and in-depth media mix will disappoint those looking for tidy answers. But then tidy answers get us nowhere in such a complex world. Wisdom, empathy, an ability to live with ambivalence and ambiguity: these are the fruits of the balanced media diet—and they will get us much further on the path of dialogue.

Will the Circle Be Too Narrow?

A while back, I volunteered to be an usher at the annual, three-day convention of our Episcopal diocese. It was not a seamless fit, to say the least. The diocesan leaders (and most of the attendees) are socially conservative; I am not. They interpret the Bible literally; I do not. I revel in a simple, silent, contemplative worship; they are loud, enjoy hourlong sermons, sing praise music, and wave their hands in the air.

Even so, Episcopalians of all stripes are generally known for a measure of decorum. So, as we prepared for the Saturday night healing service, I was *not* expecting our team leader to ask me to serve as a "catcher"— catching the people who, when prayed for as they come forward to the stage for healing, are "slain in the Spirit" and fall to the floor.

This was just a hair beyond my comfort zone. I had visions of wild, intense services, where a charismatic leader onstage would lay his hands on the supplicants before him and thunder, *"Heal!"* People would sob uncontrollably while others dropped to the floor like rocks. Legs would be lengthened, wheelchairs would be cast aside, strange tongues would be spoken—no, shouted. Not exactly the ideal scenario for simple, silent, contemplative me.

Even so, I was glad to be in a place where people need "catchers." In chapter 3, we talked about absolutists who, over time, expand their lists of "must believes" and thus shrink the circle of people with whom to dialogue. Conversely, there are few better ways to understand people—especially those with whom you disagree—than by living alongside them for a day, or a week, or regularly throughout your life.

Interesting things happen when you immerse yourself in their culture. You hear the reasoning behind their fervently held opinions. You begin to pick up their language, the meaning of their code words, their nuances of thought. You can, with some work, even think within their mind-set.

The language differences can be particularly enlightening. A college friend of mine—a radical activist and a rabble-rouser—was sitting in the campus café when the student leader of the Christian fellowship drew up a chair. An unlikelier duo you will never meet. They did, however, enjoy a friendly and heady conversation. Finally, when it came time to leave, the Christian leader said, "Hey, it's been great ministering to each other like this." To which my friend replied, "What ministering? We were just talking!" If they had had the time to explore the use of the word *ministering,* would they have discovered that they were using two words to describe the same thing?

As important as language is, however, this practice of broadening one's circle holds an even deeper lesson. When you live cheek by jowl with your "opponents," you see them in all their humanity. At that convention, I heard conservative Christians speak passionately against the blessing of same-sex couples. But I also saw them swat mosquitoes, tuck into the meat loaf, and drag themselves to bed at night. I had the privilege of swapping stories with them about our children. In short, they were conservative, they were evangelical, yes, but they were *human*. That perspective, when combined with the commitment to love we discussed in chapter 4, naturally softens the heart toward dialogue.

There is a certain magic in this circle broadening. An elder at one of my former churches expressed it well: "I can sit here and argue with you all night, and at the end of the meeting I want to throttle you. Then, two weeks later, I'll find myself at another meeting, espousing *exactly* the same points you put forward." Some may interpret this as the product of a weak will and waffling convictions, but I see it as the natural process of living together: we cannot help but rub off on one another. (More accurately, we cannot help but *rewire* one another: neuroscientists have discovered that interpersonal relationships can actually reshape our brain circuitry.)[3] The more we expose ourselves to different people and their ideas, then, the more open we become to active dialogue.

So did I become a "catcher"? Alas, after a great deal of thought, I couldn't quite bring myself to catch swooning people. I could, however, escort them off the stage once they got up—many are unsteady on their feet after such an experience—so I stayed through a good part of the service doing just that. What I saw surprised me: no shrieking, no flailing, just a quiet prayer of healing for person after person, in a spirit of reverence and, yes, decorum. I was more than surprised; I was actually blessed. The people with whom I wrestled over controversial issues displayed a gentleness and compassion that I found moving. To cap off the experience, one of the evening's keynote speakers (a conservative in her own right) watched me steadily as I helped people off the stage; later she pulled me aside to tell me I had the "gift of mercy." At that point, we were not enemies or opponents—just two people giving and receiving an encouraging word. All of this opened me a bit more for my next encounter with the "other side."

Across the Border

And yet, for all that blessing, consider just how small a step attending the convention was. The participants, though diverse of thought on certain issues, were overwhelmingly white. All spoke American English, and all lived in upstate New York. All these traits describe me as well.

How much could we learn if we pushed out further?

Exponentially more, as it turns out. When we delve into another culture entirely, we quickly discover an incredible diversity of viewpoints. What seems self-evident to white Anglo-Americans might be completely foreign to a South African matriarch, or an aboriginal hunter in Australia, or a young professional in Singapore. We cannot help but begin to see our personal worldview as one among many.

This leads to some interesting moral quandaries. A sociology professor at my Christian alma mater once asked us our thoughts on the hospitality customs of certain Alaskan peoples. To show a proper welcome, the man of the household invites a male guest to sleep with his wife; rejecting this offer is a great insult. How would those of us who treasure monogamy react in such a situation?

And what does this mean for our understanding of universal truths? One could, for instance, see the aforementioned example as an affront to women, and vast swaths of our planet's people take (correctly, I believe) the rights of women to be a universal. Does that mean there is no room for the customs of these Alaskan peoples, or other customs that we hold to be repugnant? We will examine this a bit more closely at the end of the chapter. For now, though, the lesson is clear: as we transcend our borders, our eyes open to the myriad ways of thinking beyond those borders, and we see our place in the universe—as one person among billions, as one culture among hundreds—ever more clearly.

So how do we go about this? The steps are easy to describe, but not always easy to accomplish. On the grandest level, travel abroad— even better, living abroad—can immerse us in an entirely different way of thinking and living. For evidence of this, strike up a conversation with anyone who has sojourned in the developing world; inevitably, you will hear something like "I had no idea what *real* poverty was until I went abroad."

That experience was particularly poignant for a community college professor I interviewed several years ago. He was teaching American literature in Budapest for a semester, part of a program to strengthen education in emerging economies. "One of my Hungarian students had me over for dinner," he told me. "I showed her a picture of my house in America. It's a basic two-story colonial with an attached garage. She looked at it and asked, 'Which part do you live in?' Owning the whole house was inconceivable to her."[4]

Not all the observations are that striking, but they can open our eyes nonetheless. My father-in-law, who in his eighties walks rather hesitantly, flew into Cape Town for a visit to South Africa. At the airport, he was promptly whisked into a wheelchair by an African who appeared out of nowhere. This attendant had no badge, no credentials, no "official" logo; neither did his equipment. He was just a guy who, somehow, had managed to scrounge up a wheelchair. But he wheeled my father-in-law to his destination and earned a generous tip for his efforts. In that small episode, my father-in-law glimpsed the ingenuity and entrepreneurship that millions of poor South Africans use every day just to survive.

Of course, there are different ways to travel, and thus different degrees of immersion. The longer your stay, the more different the culture from your own, the more direct your contact with those who live in it, the greater the opportunity for awakening to the difference. A weeklong guided tour through England will likely broaden an American's perspective far less than a year of volunteer work in Sudan. But both are legitimate ways of pushing out the boundaries, as long as they help us make contact with the authentic culture.

Needless to say, this sort of travel can involve considerable time and expense. Fortunately, there are other ways to push the limits. Stays in Canada or Mexico can be an eye-opening experience. Trips to other regions of the United States—or from one's home in the suburbs to the inner city, or vice versa—can surprise with unusual twists on what we think is a monolithic culture. You might see it in everything from the sublime to the trivial: from racial dynamics to wedding traditions to the names for carbonated beverages in contiguous regions (*pop* in western New York, *soda* in eastern New York, *tonic* in Massachusetts).

Even if you can't leave your own region, however, there are still ways to cross the border, albeit virtually. Learning a new language, for instance: because our language both shapes and emanates from our unique cultural way of thinking, immersion in another language automatically immerses us in a different mind-set. When someone utters a foreign phrase and then says, "There's no exact English translation," she's really saying, "There's no way to *think* about this in English." To understand the concept behind the phrase, we have to enter the language.

The examples of this are endless. Two French verbs, *vousvoyer* and *tutoyer,* have to do with addressing someone in the second person singular. Why two verbs? Because, whereas English has one form for this purpose (*you*), French has two: *vous* (formal) and *tu* (informal). *Vousvoyer,* then, means "to use the formal *vous* form when addressing someone," while *tutoyer* refers to the use of the informal *tu.* Making the *vousvoyer-tutoyer* decision is not unlike deciding whether to call one's neighbor Mr. Rhys-Stanton or Steve. But the subtle distinction of these two verbs would be completely lost on those who do not speak French.[5]

Even more simply, we can borrow from the circle-broadening insights of the previous section to transcend borders. Befriending people from other cultures can bring those cultures directly to you, if the friendship develops beyond the casual. Taking part in intercultural events or online communities may bring you face-to-face with thinking from widely different parts of the world.

So can volunteering outside your comfort zone. Imagine growing up in Los Angeles with adults who deal in Mexican jokes and stereotypes. Under these conditions, you might look at a homeless Mexican on the street and automatically think, "Oh, of course he doesn't have a job. He's Mexican." Now imagine you're asked to volunteer in a shelter that *serves* homeless Mexicans. You might begin to wonder about each person you encounter, what his story is, how he became homeless. You learn that the reality of being Mexican is far more complex than a stereotype can express. Even more important, you learn to see each person not as Mexican, but as unique. The only way to learn more about that uniqueness (and broaden your perspective still further) is to listen to that person—and we are back to dialogue again.

Clearly, the steps can be big or small, and the impact may vary accordingly. The key is to do what we can. By stepping across borders, literally or virtually, we provide ourselves with cross-cultural fodder to absorb and ponder. If we have prepared our souls to receive it, as discussed in chapter 4, the effect can be profound indeed.

Learning the Wrong Lessons

In the course of broadening our perspective, we will undoubtedly come across viewpoints so offensive that, for better or worse, we are tempted to think them unworthy of consideration. Should we consider them, and if so, what are we to make of them? In other words, how do we take away the right lessons from each encounter?

Let's say your balanced media diet includes a three-year subscription to *Dictator Today*.[6] In its pages, you get the view from the tyrant's side: perhaps an interview with Robert Mugabe, a retrospective on Stalin's contributions to Soviet society, or a posthumous editorial by Saddam Hussein. As you read, you learn about the backgrounds of these dictators and why they might have become who they are. Even more frightening, you begin to see the rationale behind their actions. What do you do with these newfound insights? Are you at risk of taking a morally reprehensible position—or at least learning to tolerate the reprehensible?

The question is hardly trivial. Philosopher Edmund Burke's eighteenth-century warning throws the stakes into stark relief: "The only thing necessary for the triumph of evil is for good men to do nothing"—or, perhaps, to believe that evil might have a certain logic after all. For us as individuals, learning such lessons may be corrosive to the soul; if enough of us draw the same lessons, the outcome may be catastrophic.

At first glance, our artificial example should make the questions moot. No sane person can condone the oppression of entire populations by one ruthless person or a powerful elite. Therefore, anti-dictatorship must be a universal value. And yet look at the revival of Stalin's image in modern-day Russia, particularly among the young. "After the anarchy that followed the collapse of the Soviet Union in 1991," wrote Nina L. Khrushcheva, the great-granddaughter of Nikita Khrushchev and a teacher of international affairs at the New School, "it turned out that Russians didn't like their new, 'free' selves. Having for centuries had no sense of self-esteem outside the state, we found ourselves wanting our old rulers back, the rulers who provided a sense of order, inspired patriotic fervor and the belief that we were a great nation."[7]

The picture gets even muddier when we start examining other values that we take as universal. Is democracy the best way for *all* people to govern themselves? Is life on this earth *always* preferable to death? (What about people in persistent vegetative states or excruciating, untreatable pain?) If organizations that we call "terrorist" are evil, how do we respond when they provide social services to the poor, as Hamas does in Gaza? (Clearly, though, we cannot call Hamas entirely good: otherwise, how do we explain its commitment to the extinction of Israel?)

Brilliant minds have debated these issues for years and will continue to do so. Often—especially when reason alone fails to resolve them—the quest for answers takes us into a familiar place: the realm of faith. The view from that realm is more reassuring, because faith gives us a coherent cognitive framework from which to think through these issues, even where it does not provide absolute answers. Moreover, this is true of all the major faith traditions, for they all agree on the moral values—such as compassion, support for those who are less fortunate, and the importance of relationship—that stand in opposition to evil and oppression.

Now add the work of the soul to this cognitive framework of faith. As you'll recall from chapter 4, the nearer we draw to God, the more room we give God to transform us. This inner transformation, which shapes the whole way we think and act, aligns us more closely with the divine orientation toward compassion and virtue. Rather than simply take a position *in favor of* good, we *become* good. In this way, our transformed inner selves serve as the unshakable core against which we hold certain ideas and experiences up to scrutiny. And by serving as our anchor, this core allows us the freedom to explore *all* points of view without fear.

Here's an example: I have practiced Christianity for more than thirty-five years and contemplative prayer for more than fifteen. All those hours of silent prayer and liturgical prayer and Bible reading and listening to sermons have drawn me closer to the God at the core of the faith. As a result, I look at various events—in the world, in my life, in human his-tory—and can identify them immediately with the God I've come to know. Conversely, I examine other events and see a portrait of a God I do not recognize. It doesn't, as I like to say, "smell like God."

This applies, I believe, even to the pages of scripture. I read the book of Joshua, in which God orders the people of Israel to wipe out the Canaanites—a reprehensible act by the standards of many people—and encounter an understanding of God with which I am not familiar. I use my personal experience with God as a benchmark to assess the Joshua story, as I use it to assess the Arab Spring (an exhilarating collective cry for freedom and human dignity) and the attempts to crush it. At the same time, that closeness to God allows me the freedom to question what I see, even in the scriptures of my faith tradition, without concern for "losing my faith."

Does this mean my personal connection with God is the only arbiter of what I deem good or evil? Not at all. Remember, I'm only one person with one limited perspective. So I search the scriptures of my faith (and of other faiths). I listen to the traditions of the Christian Church. I hold up truth claims to the measures of reason. All those inputs—scripture, tradition, reason, experience—interact together to provide greater insight. (It is, in fact, a sort of internal dialogue.) But my relationship with God is what keeps me centered and sane amid the cacophony of external voices claiming "the truth."

By cooperating in the work of our soul, then, we give ourselves the clearest possible perspective from which to view all viewpoints for what they are, deepen our understanding of all people, yet remain fixed on God's will. And by studying the reprehensible in this context, we better equip ourselves to counteract it.

By observing and assessing from the core of our souls, we put our-selves in the best position to learn the right lessons. And no one should underestimate the importance of that. "We should be careful to get out of an experience only the wisdom that is in it—and stop there," Mark Twain wrote, "lest we be like the cat that sits down on a hot stove-lid. She will never sit down on a hot stove-lid again—and that is well; but also she will never sit down on a cold one any more."[8]

The Step into Dialogue

There are so many personal benefits to living dialogue as a habit of the heart—to tilling the soil of our souls and extending our perspective far beyond ourselves. As we see our place in the universe, we let go of our need to control and strive and attain. We become content to lead our lives in concert with God, which brings (to paraphrase Jesus) a peace that the world cannot give. The world around us opens our eyes; the commitment to love opens our hearts. The things that block us from becoming our best selves fall away. We find ourselves more joyful and more curious. We become, in a word, larger.

These benefits are invaluable all by themselves. But there is, of course, more to the story. By making us larger, they energize us for a larger purpose: to pursue the dialogue that we as humans, and the world as a whole, so urgently need. Let us now discuss the way to begin that dialogue.

FOR YOUR CONSIDERATION ...

1. Take a fresh look at your news sources. Evaluate them from as many perspectives as you can think of: conservative versus liberal, social conservative versus economic conservative, atheist versus evangelical, and so on. What are the strengths of your media diet? What news sources would help you balance it?

2. What foreign country fascinates you? What would it take for you to travel there, to learn its language, or to explore it online?

3. How many of your good friends are not like you? In what ways? How could you broaden your circle to broaden your perspective?

4. What part of your community lies the furthest outside your comfort zone? What would happen if you volunteered in that area or with those people?

5. With what in this chapter do you disagree? Why?

Making Dialogue Happen

I once had a circle of friends who were wild about Hermann Hesse, the German author and thinker. One of their most cherished orthodoxies concerned the order in which Hesse's books were to be read. You should begin with *Siddhartha,* move on to *Damien,* step up to some of Hesse's other novels, and only then, when you were truly ready, immerse yourself in *Magister Ludi.* In other words, there was a prescribed path, and you could not move on to the next step until you had completed the one before. Only after following the progression in order could you fully understand Hermann Hesse.

Dialogue is nothing like this. There is no "ladder of dialogical perfection" that we must climb before truly discoursing with other people. On the contrary: in the way of dialogue, we have dialogue along the way. How could it be otherwise? We cannot put off the latest tiff with our partner, or the current tension at work, or global discussion of climate change until the soil of our soul is perfectly tilled. The more we till, of course, the more effective our dialogue will be—and the more we can model the way of dialogue for others. But here as with so many other human activities, the best way to start is simply to start.

But how?

A Seat at the Dialogue Table

When I was in high school, our cafeteria had a French table—a lunch area where you could speak only French and nothing else. The idea behind it was clear: you could take all the classes and language labs you wanted, but unless you immersed yourself in a real-life French-speaking situation, your knowledge would never rise above the level of theory. The more proficient speakers would serve as models of pronunciation, idiom, and confidence; the less proficient could practice their skills in a (relatively) safe environment. To put it simply, French at my high school was not just taught, but caught.

Dialogue is the same way. When we station ourselves at the "dialogue table," in places where dialogue is spoken, we see what it looks like in real life. We learn from those who have already prepared their souls and honed their skills. Just as important, we catch their spirit—the openness, thoughtfulness, and gentleness that often accompany people of dialogue. Gradually, once we have heard enough to understand the tone and style of the group, we join the conversation ourselves and develop *our* skills.

But where can you find these "dialogue tables"? Fortunately, it is not a matter of flying cross-country to attend a dialogue conference (though that may prove valuable, too). Quite the opposite: it makes sense to start with the people you already know and trust—a close friend, family member, or work colleague whose approach to ideas you admire. Check your mental contact list. Have you ever been in a meeting and noticed a colleague seeking common ground between two opposing sides? Does one of your friends always take what's said in stride, considering it carefully and with respect for the speaker? Who serves as the peacemaker in your family—not the person who avoids conflict by "smoothing everything over," but the one who honestly helps family members sort out their feelings? Is there someone whose very presence makes you relax inside?

One of my most treasured friends fits this description to a T. Bill is soft-spoken, gentle by nature, and a superb listener. No matter how outrageous the idea on the table, he always approaches it with respect, remaining silent and turning it over in his mind before offering a thought or two on which to build an authentic dialogue. In the course of the ensuing discussion, he gives the idea its due and goes out of his way to honor the other person's responses, even when he does not agree. As a result, our discussions over the years have helped me see new ways of thinking that I didn't know existed.

Now there's no reason to stride purposefully up to your chosen dialogue partner and announce, "I would like to have a dialogue with you." Instead, invite her to lunch. Slip in a question about an issue or perspective during a conversation. Ask her advice on a particular situation. Just like that, you've created your own dialogue table.

Before you know it, the dynamics of my old high school French table take hold. You start to pick up on the cues of your selected dialogist. You observe her tone, her careful word choice, her mannerisms, her thought patterns. Quite naturally, you mirror them. And *naturally* is the word: studies have shown an unconscious tendency to imitate others' movements and speech patterns when we converse with them.[1] Of course, because you are a participant in this dialogue, you will be practicing what you pick up.

That last point is critical to the whole exercise. Getting to dialogue proficiency is just like getting to Carnegie Hall: it takes practice, practice, practice. The more people you engage in this way, the more variety in style you will encounter, and the more proficient you will become in your own approach to dialogue. Along the way, many of the fruits we discussed in earlier chapters will accrue to you as well: these repeated dialogues will likely spark your curiosity, introduce you to viewpoints you might never have considered, expand your worldview, reveal the essential humanity of those who disagree with you, and bring clarity to your image of yourself as one person among many, with one perspective among many.

Your practice does not have to stop with one-on-one dialogues. Seek out groups that promote dialogue by their very nature. Interfaith alliances and discussions are particularly valuable here: the tension between Islam and the West has inspired many of these initiatives, and they provide a forum for people oriented toward dialogue to both practice their skills and contribute to the general conversation. Online discussion groups are important for gathering geographically dispersed people around a common issue.

Of course, some groups are better at dialogue than others. The challenge is to find groups whose participants are civil, mutually respectful, and fearless in probing even sensitive topics without rancor. Make sure that your chosen group, while exploring common issues, does not approach them from a common *perspective:* a group of single-issue partisans might get on well, but its value in preparing you for dialogue with opposing views is severely limited.

The dynamics of one-on-one dialogue apply here, too. The tone and manner of participants in dialogue groups is caught more than taught. That is why many online discussion boards suggest that you lurk for a while before posting: it gives you time to absorb the tone and style of the group.

Rules to Talk By

Earlier I noted that you can spend hundreds of hours in classroom and language lab, but without real-world experience, you won't become truly proficient in your language of choice. The converse is also true. You can eat at the French table every day for years, but unless you learn vocabulary, syntax, verb tenses, and all the other formalities of the language, you will get nowhere. To practice the rules, you have to *know* the rules.

So, too, with dialogue. As we have discussed, practice will make you a better dialogist, but without the ground rules, how will you know what you are practicing? Understanding the basics helps you to become more proficient more quickly, avoid common mistakes, and dialogue with more confidence.

Dozens of books have been written on conflict resolution and the process of dialogue, so there is no need to cover all the rules here. The following basics, however, will help you get started in your quest to make dialogue happen.

Suspend your preconceptions. As we have observed throughout this book, our default setting as human beings is to listen to another through the filter of our own ingrained perspectives and values. While we cannot escape them completely, we *can* do our best to set them aside, clearing our minds and hearts to listen more intently to the other's unvarnished perspective.

I once took part in a writers' group with an accomplished astrologer. The minute I heard of her profession, I could feel my defenses going up—the vestige of my evangelical Christian past, during which I had learned to equate astrology with evil. Later, as we drove to an event, we discussed her approach to astrology. If I had left that conservative filter in place, I would have spent the whole time "defending myself" against this "evil" and trying to find holes in the theory behind it. By laying the filter aside, I heard so much more: the vast gulf between serious astrology and the tabloid version, the practical aims and goals of the profession, and other things that, taken together, painted a portrait of a viable alternative worldview. In short, what I heard about astrology from an astrologer was far different from what I had heard from preachers. Only by setting aside the preacher's voice in my head could I begin to grasp the reality of the astrologer's world.

The spiritual practices we discussed in chapter 4 play a major role in getting us to suspend our preconceptions. When we practice humility and openness on a regular basis, when we make a habit of pursuing truth no matter how much it might contradict our own cherished beliefs, we more readily see those beliefs as comprising one system among many. That perspective allows us to loosen our grip on our own belief system, which, in turn, fosters a greater willingness to hear and assess new ideas on their own merits. This does not mean we accept these new ideas carte blanche; it does mean we give them the consideration they deserve.

Absorb, then project. In his book *You Are the Message,* political consultant and FOX News president Roger Ailes describes a communication technique that has value for dialogue as well.[2] When you walk into a gathering, Ailes advises, first spend a minute "absorbing": taking the temperature of the room to gauge the moods and sensibilities of the people therein. Only after doing so should you enter the fray. This puts you on the same wavelength as the other members of the group, and you will be able to interact with them more effectively.

If you think about the whole spectrum of social situations in which we find ourselves, that makes a great deal of sense. You wouldn't, for instance, want to go laughing and joking into a room whose participants had just heard that a beloved friend had died. By picking up on the ambience first, you can act with greater sensitivity toward the people gathered there.

This principle applies to any dialogue, but particularly those conducted in groups. When people gather for an interfaith dialogue or a civic discussion or a family tribunal, the information you glean from "absorbing" can help you shape the dialogue to the needs and sensitivities of the participants. Thus shaped, the dialogue can then foster greater trust and avoid needless obstacles that might create detours into hostility or misunderstanding.

While the absorb-project dynamic is ideal for the first few moments of a dialogue, its usefulness doesn't stop there. Over lunch in a sports bar, my friend Mary and I were discussing a serious family situation (her mother suffers from Alzheimer's disease) when her phone rang: Mom's doctor had called to discuss a particular aspect of her health. Mary excused herself and took the call while I watched football on one of the TVs. When Mary returned, I was a bit absorbed in the game, and because the gate between my brain and my mouth does not work well, I referred to it when Mary returned to the table. If, instead, I had absorbed first, I would have seen that she was near tears, and I would have shut up and listened to her. In the end, my faux pas didn't sidetrack the conversation, but it could have.

The lesson is clear: it never hurts to take the temperature of a dialogue—first, last, and always. That, in turn, feeds into a related skill:

Listen deeply. The word *listening,* like *love,* has lost a good deal of its full meaning. We think of listening as paying attention just long enough to formulate a response or "get the gist" of the other person's comments. As a result, we may miss the full import of those comments; that leads us to misunderstand one another and respond to what we *think* we hear.

Deep listening, by contrast, requires a clear mind and a total focus on the other person. It allows for reflection after someone speaks to properly weigh what he has said. In my experiences with the Clearness Committee framework, which we discussed in chapter 3, the proceedings took place with regular silences between question and answer, one statement and the next. No one needed to impose these silences from on high; the context of listening almost automatically produced them.

How do we get to this clear mind and total focus on the other? At first glance, it is a simple matter of paying attention—but paying attention is not so simple amid the pace of daily life in the Western world. Here, as with suspending our preconceptions, the spiritual practices we discussed in chapter 4 can help. A fringe benefit of silent prayer and meditation, especially, is that they clear away the distractions of the day and enable us to focus on one simple thing. Meditation on the breath, for example—a gentle but single-minded focus on our inhaling and exhaling—empties our minds by centering our attention on one of our most automatic, rhythmic biological functions. When our minds are clear and our hearts are quiet, they are open as well, and more oriented toward listening. And while clearing the mind, these exercises also *train* the mind: having learned to focus on one thing for a sustained period, we can transfer that ability to focusing on one person in dialogue.

We have touched on this before, but it bears repeating: all this listening, like the dialogue in which it occurs, takes time—at least enough to allow the participants to hear and be heard fully, think through what has been said, explore issues, and make progress together. By contrast, I have seen countless meeting agendas in which a serious, complex issue, requiring depth of thought and listening, is given ten minutes at the end of the meeting, when everyone just wants to move on to the next appointment. In a similar vein, why do business or association retreats, in which the participants may be planning the course of their organization for the next year, take only three hours at the end of the workday?

Ask questions. We can throw our preconceptions to the wind, empty our minds and our hearts of all distractions, focus our sustained attention on the other person, and *still* misunderstand her. This is perfectly natural. As we have seen elsewhere in this book, so many factors shape our understanding and use of specific words—factors intensely personal to ourselves—that we can easily hear a turn of phrase and assign it a meaning that the speaker never intended. If that can happen with individual words and phrases, how much more can we miss in longer, more complex stretches of dialogue?

To fix this issue, questions may be the most effective tool in our verbal toolbox. We might ask precisely how the speaker is defining certain terms: as much flak as Bill Clinton received about his endless parsing of words during the Monica Lewinsky scandal—"It depends what the meaning of *is* is"—this kind of precision can truly help us understand one another more clearly. We might also try repeating the speaker's ideas back to him: "What I hear you saying is [insert your understanding here]. Is that what you meant?"

In the process, we might uncover entirely new depths of insight that had never occurred to the speaker. During one particularly difficult phase of our dating relationship, Prudence asked me what I meant when I said, "I love you." At first I gave her what I thought was a reasonable answer, but it wasn't good enough for her. She persisted with the question, and that forced me not only to articulate my use of *love* more clearly, but also to develop my understanding of the whole concept. If she had not pressed that line of questioning so doggedly, I might not have come to understand love in a fuller way—and I certainly could not have given her the depth of love she needed from the relationship.

The form of these questions is just as important as their content: they need to be "answer-neutral"—that is, with no bias whatsoever toward a specific solution, position, or line of thought. The rules of the Clearness Committee prohibit questioners from asking any question with an answer already in mind or sharing a thought from their own experience. That precludes leading questions or solutions: for instance, "Don't you think …?" or "Wouldn't you agree …?" or "Maybe you could …" Also off-limits is "When I had this problem, I solved it by [solution here]. Would that work for you?" The entire goal is to help the "focus person" plumb the depths of her own issue, not to lead her on to something that may or may not spring up from within her soul.[3]

While the Clearness Committee uses these rules for a specific purpose, they apply to dialogue of any type. Only answer-neutral questions allow the speaker the intellectual and emotional space in which to speak freely.

By now, you might be thinking that crafting these questions is considerably harder work than it first appears. You would be right. This is another reason that time and reflection are so important to the process of dialogue: difficult tasks tend to take more time by their very nature. In this case, the hard work involves a good dose of our next rule:

Watch your language. The precision of language that we use in our questions is a must throughout the entire dialogue. In part, we overcome the various differences in our understanding of words by defining, and drawing on, the shared meaning of those words. There's not a lot of room for "whatever" or "you know what I mean" in dialogue.

The less we have in common with our dialogue partners, the more precise our language must be. If an evangelical Christian is talking with another evangelical Christian, they might be able to use the word *sin* without taking the time to define it. That is not likely if the same Christian is in dialogue with a Buddhist, whose faith tradition places far less emphasis on sin. When writing brochures for an international audience, I was always advised to use the English language in as straightforward a manner as possible, because readers might easily miss the significance of an American cultural idiom (just as I, with my rudimentary knowledge of French, might be able to understand all the words in a Renault brochure but still miss the meaning of certain expressions).

Unfortunately, it's not even that simple: even the words you think require no definition can surprise you. In the space of one week, I used *silo* in three separate conversations to indicate an environment in which various parts of an organization did not speak with one another. None of my listeners understood the term. In two cases the miscommunication could perhaps be explained: the listeners were an attorney in state service and an accomplished librarian, so I simply figured that *silo* was business jargon, unfamiliar to them. But the third person was a highly sophisticated businessperson in a graphic design firm. Clearly, it is difficult to overestimate the importance of choosing one's words carefully, no matter who the audience.

But the value of precision does not lie only in communicating our thoughts and hearing our colleagues more effectively. Precision also allows us to get past the typical language used to frame issues—language that can, by its very overuse, begin to obscure the nuance and complexity of the issue itself. And because this typical language is sometimes inflammatory, choosing other words can move us beyond anger into a calmer space where we can consider the issues with a clearer mind.

Once we do that, we can start exploring the complexities and see where they take us. What might happen, for instance, if Republicans stopped referring to "tax and spend" Democrats and instead offered more nuanced critiques of certain economic plans? What if Democrats could get beyond the epithet "tax breaks for big corporations" and explain exactly *why* those tax breaks are necessarily a bad thing? With these explanations in hand, those of us who know less about the issues could weigh the nuances on both sides and form more intelligent opinions about the truth of the matter. And isn't that one goal of dialogue: to pursue the truth?

Seek common ground. It is much harder to demonize your dialogue partner when you realize how much the two of you have in common. This can occur on two levels. First, and most fundamental, is our common humanity. During our visit to South Africa, Prudence and I made the acquaintance of a Xhosa woman who was on retreat for her fiftieth birthday. One of our most delightful moments with her came when she explained part of the reason for her retreat: her teenage daughter was driving her crazy. Instantly we had a bond that obliterated the thousands of miles between our homelands and our cultures. If we had been in dialogue with her about some contentious issue, that common bond (and the continuing awareness of it) would humanize us in one another's eyes— allowing us to explore the issue together rather than debate it.

We can also seek common ground on the issue at hand. At first— especially on issues where passions run high—this may seem impossible. But consider several of these issues. Don't proponents and opponents of gay marriage share a profound reverence for the institution of marriage itself? This is encouraging news in a culture where divorce is so rampant and many are afraid to make a life commitment. Can we say that both sides of the abortion debate share at least one common goal: to reduce the incidence of abortion? It is hard to imagine even the most ardent "pro-choice" advocate wanting to *increase* the number.

When we seek out common ground, we often find that we agree far more than we disagree. Above all, we see that we share many of the same struggles, cares, and dreams. This puts the issue in a larger context and, in so doing, takes the emotional thunder out of the dispute.

Reframe the issue. This is the practical handmaiden to seeking common ground, and it is especially valuable when dialogue stalls. As the blind men have taught us, nearly any issue can be approached from multiple perspectives. The trick is to step back, look for a different frame of reference, and see where the new view takes you. "What if we looked at it *this* way?" is the tool in your dialogue toolbox to spark this process.

In the business of advertising, this ability to reframe can separate the great creative thinkers from the merely good ones. Industry icon Howard Gossage illustrated this when writing about the "ability to behold," which he believed was a key to creativity:

> It is seeing a hundred horses run by and saying, "Hey, that one there is a zebra!" … What happens from here on depends on what sort of person the beholder is. The conservative beholder might say, "What the hell is that zebra doing in there?" … The pragmatic beholder might ask, "What the hell do you do with a zebra?" … The imaginative or zebra-oriented beholder—and there are quite a few of them around—might ask, "What are we going to do with those ninety-nine horses?" These are the people who are always coming to me for jobs.… But the type of beholder I rather fancy not only is imaginative and practical but has a plan, too. He says, "OK, here's what we're going to do with those ninety-nine non-zebras."[4]

Approaching the issue from the non-zebra perspective might reveal an entirely different, and more fruitful, line of thinking. A mainline Protestant church in a severe budget crunch might look hopelessly at the numbers and see no way out. "We've cut x hundred from the hospitality committee," the trustees might say, "and y hundred from the music program, but we're still $20,000 short. And we just did a big stewardship campaign, so our members are tapped out." However, what would happen if the trustees brainstormed new revenue streams? Does the church really need three pastors, or can it make do with one? Even better, what if they decided to sell the building?

None of these options should be pursued lightly, but reframing along these lines may open up other opportunities. Perhaps, without a building to constrict them, the church members decide to rent a modest storefront in a poor neighborhood. Maybe that leads to entirely new ministries and a reenergized membership. Perhaps the layoff of clergy, however painful, might inspire the laypeople to step up and develop their leadership gifts.

The point, of course, is not to create a model for struggling congregations. It is simply to illustrate just how much of an impact reframing might have on the progress of dialogue.

Here again, our work of the soul can bear much fruit. We have already explored how the practice of humility, openness, prayer, travel, and the other suggestions in this book serve to broaden our perspective. The broader our perspective, the more open we become to unusual ideas—and the more likely we are to approach something "outside the box" with curiosity and careful consideration.

Lighten up. Dialogues can get very serious and very intense. They involve sustained concentration, reflection, and listening, all of which require considerable work. Occasionally, therefore, we need a reminder that (in nearly all cases) the fate of the world does *not* depend on our getting this dialogue, in this place, at this time, absolutely correct. On these occasions, humor is nothing less than a gift from God.

As our burgeoning house church wrestled with the momentous decision of whether to split into smaller groups, the discussions often turned contentious, and we turned to euphemisms—*divide, bud, grow*—to soften the discussion. In one nerve-racking meeting, where the tension hung over the room like heat in July, one of our most passionate and funniest members started in on a rant. He had had it with the euphemisms and the pleasantries and the dancing around the issue, he said, "and all because we're afraid to utter that one four-letter word—*split!*" The entire room dissolved into howls of laughter, and for a while, at least, we could talk with one another again.

As I wrote in a poem many years ago, "Our work is serious; don't take it seriously." If we can hold that paradox in mind when pursuing our dialogue—and laugh a little along the way—we can be freer to make mistakes, stumble over our words, explore trains of thought that go nowhere. Ironically, that freedom may help the dialogue flow more freely.

Yes, dialogue is important business, and we want to approach it with all the precision, focused listening, and thoughtfulness we can muster. But by lightening up, we give ourselves permission to be human, too. And our common humanity may just bind us together more than anything we can say.

Keeping the Goal in Mind

Dialogue is not about winning. In fact, it would be difficult to define just what "winning a dialogue" would look like. If we come to an agreement on a course of action or uncover a new and helpful insight, haven't we *both* won? If one of us contributes deeper insights than the other, don't we *both* benefit? And who is to say that a single sentence, perhaps even one offered in jest, cannot turn the dialogue's whole course around?

Similarly, dialogue is not about changing the other person's mind. That belongs to the realm of persuasion and, to a lesser extent, debate. Besides, if we enter dialogue with a clear mind and an open heart, just what are we changing the other person's mind *to,* anyway? The work of the soul tends to clear out, or at least soften, the entrenched opinions that, in other situations, we might want to convince the other person of.

No, dialogue is about something else. As we have seen in previous chapters, it is about seeking truth, seeing the world from another's viewpoint, coming to a deeper mutual understanding, learning to love more deeply. When action is necessary, we aim for a mutually agreeable way of proceeding.

Dialogues tend to involve sensitive issues with deep emotion on all sides. The practical rules and techniques described here and in other books will help us navigate toward our goal. But when sensitivities are offended and things get contentious, keeping the goal in mind—and always upholding the commitment to love—will help us regain perspective, see the humanity of the other participants, and press on with fresh courage.

FOR YOUR CONSIDERATION ...

1. Whom did you choose for your first dialogue partner? Why?

2. Think of an issue about which you are wildly passionate. Now
    imagine sitting across the table from someone who believes
    exactly the opposite of the way you do. How could you re-
    frame the issue to arrive at common ground? Does this reveal
    any new insights about the issue at hand?

3. Think back to the last time someone completely misunder-
    stood a word or phrase you thought was common knowledge.
    How did the person react? How did you react? What did you
    do to clarify what you meant? How would you handle this
    kind of situation the next time it arose?

4. What might happen if, the next time you meet with some-
    one who dislikes your opinions, you start by discussing the
    funniest lines you've ever heard in a meeting? How could
    you build on that to make progress in your dialogue with that
    person?

5. With what in this chapter do you disagree? Why?

Dialogue Unbound

Two people sit down over coffee to discuss an issue. One speaks precisely while the other listens. When the speaker has said his peace, the other person reflects a bit, allows the comments to percolate into her opinions, and then speaks just as precisely and respectfully. They go on like this for an hour. At that point, they have found common ground, built mutual trust, and laid the foundation for their next dialogue. They embrace warmly and part ways.

This is a wonderful way to conduct dialogue. But it is not the only way.

Dialogue can take strange turns. The road to "progress" may include outright reversals. We get exhausted; our words get sharp. We lose track of what we're talking about. We sense that there is some disconnect but cannot put our finger on it. Every now and then, the issue goes away—or morphs into something very different. And on some occasions, we can go no further. That does not mean the dialogue has failed. Sometimes the fruit it bears crops up in unexpected places.

What does all this look like? And what do we do when dialogue hits the skids?

Shall We Agree to Disagree?

You hear it all the time. Friends who would die for each other disagree
vehemently about animal rights. Longtime business associates squabble
over investment strategies. Parents and teens argue about tattoos. Often,
they close discussion by "agreeing to disagree."

The idea sounds wonderfully civil. By agreeing to disagree, we pledge
to respect each other's opinions and move on. We restore harmony and
concord. Or do we?

All too often, "agreeing to disagree" turns into a tacit agreement never
to speak of the issue again. But this creates problems on several fronts.
To live out such an agreement is to hold back a part of oneself from the
other person. This diminishes the relationship by definition: how can we
give ourselves fully to the other when we declare certain issues off-limits?
Moreover, the issue in dispute often influences our thoughts in other
areas; should we not speak of these either?

The agreement to disagree erects barriers in more subtle ways as well.
People change over time. Their values and beliefs evolve. Things that were
peripheral to them five years ago might gradually take center stage, or vice
versa. If we cut ourselves off from certain parts of them, how can we share
in their growth, especially if it involves those aspects on which we have
agreed to disagree?

One of my closest friends in high school had a visceral distaste for
religion. We spent hours sharing some of our deepest concerns and hidden dreams with each other; I still consider it one of the great friendships
of my life. When I underwent a conversion experience, however, she did
not want to hear about it. (It surely did not help that I embraced my
newfound faith with all the passion of a teenage zealot.) After graduation,
I visited her with my new girlfriend, also an ardent believer, but we had
little to say and our visit was short. Surely people go their separate ways
after high school, but the issue of faith had become a wedge to ensure that
this happened to us.

There is another, more practical problem with agreeing to disagree,
and we have seen it throughout this book: sometimes you have to move
the elephant. When our last word is to agree to disagree, we still have not
established enough common ground to take action on whatever issue is

before us. If we are to resolve issues like these, we must push through this civil option to authentic dialogue.

Should we eliminate "agreeing to disagree" from our vocabulary? Not at all. It can serve as an effective strategy in a number of situations. Sometimes dialogists have expended all their energy and simply need a break; agreeing to disagree provides a convenient starting point for future discussion (and allows them to push on with other things). In instances like these, however, the phrase takes on a different definition: rather than consenting never to speak of the issue again, we are agreeing to continue dialogue in general, to share our lives with one another, while being sensitive to the disagreements and how they affect the other's thinking.

We can even take agreeing to disagree one step further—by supporting one another *within* our differing viewpoints. A close friend and I share similar spiritual temperaments but hold radically different theological views. He is a scriptural literalist and a Calvinist who believes God controls everything; I believe in free will and see the Bible as full of confusing crosscurrents. At one point, we spent the better part of two years e-mailing back and forth on the nuances of these disagreements. Sometimes, though, he just wanted my opinion of his latest sermon; rather than rant about the "hot-button" items in his message (which he *knew* I disagreed with), I tried to get inside his head and react within his theological framework in a way that might help him. This also allowed us to support each other's spiritual growth even as we disagreed.

So, yes, by all means, let us agree to disagree—if that means we also agree to hold our differences lightly and continue the dialogue.

When Dialogue "Fails": Breakdown, Weariness, and Urgency

What does it mean for dialogue to fail? The obvious answer is that we do not come to agreement. But failure can take several forms—if we can call it failure at all.

Sadly, we are all too familiar with the typical breakdown in dialogue: we cut off discussion, our interaction degenerates into recrimination, and we often take up arms. For examples, look no further than the decades of strife in the Middle East. In 2000, to cite just one instance, U.S. president Bill Clinton invited the leaders of Israel and the Palestine Liberation Organization to Camp David to hammer out the details of a Mideast peace settlement. The breakdown of those talks, according to both sides, contributed to the al-Aqsa Intifada (or the "second Intifada")[1]—the upsurge in violence between Israel and the Palestinians that took more than seventy-five hundred lives.[2]

Many obstacles can stand in the way of dialogue—including simple weariness. During a long, difficult discussion, we grow weary of the struggle. Sometimes we look at the issue from every conceivable angle and keep coming up against the same fundamental disagreements. It is tempting to throw our hands in the air and quit from exhaustion.

It is also perfectly natural. Our weariness is simply the mark of our dedication to the dialogue—the seriousness with which we take the issue, the process, and the person on the other side of the table. Even successful dialogues can leave the participants breathless from the exertion. Have you ever enjoyed a particularly intense conversation with a friend, after which you feel almost light-headed and ready for a nap? "Whew!" is often heard after one of these dialogues. And why not? Dialogue takes deliberate effort, and the effort may become exhausting.

For that reason, we need to pay attention to our own energy reserves during a dialogue—and take a break when we need to. It is no failure to step back and call a hiatus or simply to let the dialogue fall quiet while we tend to other things. The one imperative here is to alert other participants, even if it's with a simple "I may not respond as quickly as I have recently." Otherwise, it is all too easy for the others to misconstrue the quiet period as hostility, which not only leaves them hurt but, in the process, creates more hurdles for further dialogue.

And what should you do with such a hiatus? Whatever nurtures your soul. I find it particularly helpful to spend time with friends who think the way I do. Their validation, whether in their words or just in their presence, helps me regain my perspective; I begin to remember that I'm *not* crazy or ignorant or going to hell, as my dialogue partner may think, but just another person with a different but legitimate perspective.

Dialogue can also "fail" when time is of the essence—whether it is or not. Sometimes a legitimate emergency precludes the use of dialogue: you don't want your EMTs discussing the many causes of heart attacks when you're in full cardiac arrest. At other times, however, the participants face a decision and perceive that further dialogue will get them nowhere. This can directly tie in to the "dialogue fatigue" we just discussed: participants feel that an issue has been "talked to death" and they simply want to "decide and move on."

This sort of decision must be carried through with extreme caution. As we discussed in chapter 7, I once belonged to a small house church that, thanks to sustained and welcome growth, had faced a crossroads. Should it divide into several churches to maintain the intimacy that was the church's hallmark? Should it retain its current form and become a larger body, thus preserving the tight bonds of affection that had grown up among so many members? Could the two structures be combined?

The discussion went on for years. Emotions on every side of the issue ran high, and occasionally tempers flared. Because the church made decisions by consensus, each member's input was weighed carefully and treated with respect. Eventually, however, the discussions broke no new ground, and the old points were simply repeated at each meeting.

One final gathering brought this to a head. Members began to express their need to make a decision and move on. Others pressed for more talk. Finally, a show of hands was taken: all members voted for a split into smaller groups—except for five or six.

What happened next was remarkable. The meeting's facilitator called on each person who voted no, invited him or her to speak one more time, and asked if there was any way he or she could live with the split. As the group became quiet, each one agreed to do so (though with extreme reluctance), and consensus was finally, if imperfectly, achieved.

You could say that these half-dozen people experienced intense pressure to give in, and that might be the case to some extent. But the commitment to consensus ran so deep within the culture of the church that the members took pains to hear their fellow members out.

The lesson here is twofold. First, when we *truly* need to act before the dialogue has run its course, we must take the step with the utmost reverence, humility, and respect for the dissenters. A flip, condescending "We know how hard this must be for you" simply will not do. Second, we must make sure, at every seeming impasse, that we *do* need to act. When someone asserts, "We just need to get on with this," the response has to be "Do we really?" Only when the answer to that question is a resounding yes—and as unanimous as possible—can we move forward.

For each rule there are many exceptions—so many, in fact, that theory can only cover them so far. After that, we need to see concrete examples of how "imperfect" dialogue plays out in the real nitty-gritty world. Let's look, then, at three examples of dialogue that have happened, and what they say to us.

Dialogue as Magic

We had come to an impasse, and the tension across the table was palpable. The two of us had agreed to cochair our professional association's scholarship fund, which involved publicizing the scholarship with a poster and a call for applications. Under normal circumstances, we would simply use the text from last year's poster. In this particular year, however, our scholarship committee had made a crucial change to the award, allowing us to offer *two* scholarships instead of one. That, together with the terms and conditions that surrounded the change, wreaked havoc with the headline. Call it *scholarship* when it's actually *scholarships*? Can we use *scholarships* when we might just offer one after all (if, for instance, only one applicant qualified for the award)? What if we left the word out of the headline?

For some time—by phone, by e-mail, and now face-to-face—we had wrangled over this, tossing around suggestions and just as quickly rejecting them. My cochair felt the word *scholarship* was absolutely necessary in the headline; I thought the wording sounded ungrammatical and didn't fully reflect the rule change. We both dug in and insisted on our position.

With the threat of terrorism and extreme poverty and the scourge of AIDS, this sounds laughably trivial. In the grand scheme of things, it certainly is. Yet what percentage of our lives is made up precisely of moments like this, decisions like this, options in which we become, perhaps, more invested than the issue is worth? Your trivial issue may be just the one that sets me off, and vice versa. My general flexibility on many issues turns into raging wild-eyed mania on issues of grammar—and my opinion, of course, is always right.

That was part of the problem in this situation. Finally, in as much of a huff as I could muster, I gave in. We parted and went back to our respective offices.

A half hour later, my cochair called me. She had come up with a totally different approach to the headline, and she thought it might solve the problem. Lo and behold, I liked it a lot. She liked it a lot. We agreed on the spot to use it as our headline.

It was also an idea we had batted around days ago.

To all appearances, at that table where we met just a half hour before, the dialogue had failed. One person just had to give in, and gracelessly at that. But this was hardly failure: indeed, the dialogue had produced the very idea that we ended up selecting as the headline. We simply needed a hiatus—a chance to walk away from the issue, breathe a bit, and regain some perspective. Then the best idea, though we had rejected it earlier, bubbled to the surface. It seemed like magic.

This, with or without the tension, is normal for the creative brainstorming process. It also illustrates how dialogue can produce resolutions in the most unexpected ways.

The Turbulent Priest

He could be prickly at times. After many years serving Episcopal churches, his theology was conservative (perhaps even medieval), and he was rigidly set in his ways. He summarily dismissed many thoughts and perspectives I found worthy of exploration. Some of his comments made me cringe. And yet, when I objected to a point in his sermon one Sunday, I could not muster the good sense to keep my mouth shut.

That led to nearly a year's worth of e-mail discussion on all manner of things spiritual. We exchanged views on evangelism and the authority of scripture. We wrestled over the modern scholars and the literal truth (or lack thereof) of the creeds that express Christianity's foundational truths. We discussed the state of our own local congregation.

An academic exercise? Not even close. It was perhaps no coincidence that this priest came to our church when I was in a pivotal but delicate phase of reevaluating my beliefs. A church book discussion had introduced me to the historical-critical-anthropological view of scripture, as espoused by scholars like Marcus Borg and John Dominic Crossan of the Jesus Seminar. I lunched with fellow congregants who had no use for a physical resurrection of Christ or his death as atonement for sins. At the same time, after decades of recoiling from the Church's evangelical wing, I found myself wanting to repair old wounds. My mind would formulate approaches to this doctrine or that doctrine; I would wrestle with whether the events in Jesus's life were factually true, or *had* to be factually true to make the whole system work.

All this wrestling (with which I often drove myself to distraction) intensified my longtime tendency to pay attention to authority figures in the Church—not in slavish devotion but simply because we think about the same things and they're more educated than I am. Into this situation walked a conservative, combative old priest.

As you could guess, the ensuing year of discussion was not all peaches and cream. About three months in, the priest's e-mails took a more strident tone. At certain points I grew exhausted with the toil of rebutting arguments, especially when they were harshly worded. I didn't see that the dialogue was giving the priest anything new to think about (which perhaps reflected his more advanced education in theology). Is dialogue even worth the effort when one party gets nothing out of it?

In short, there were times when I thought the whole exercise was pointless. Then I'd look through our old e-mails and realize I could not be more wrong.

We've discussed how the very conduct of dialogue—our simple presence with a person who disagrees with us—can shape our views. This particular dialogue was shaping mine. Certain tenets of the historical-critical scholars left me vaguely uneasy; the dialogue not only allowed me to articulate the reasons why, but also (because the priest and I agreed on these points) gave me a safe place to do so freely. By continually dialoguing with the priest and my more progressive friends, I gradually saw my own beliefs emerge in a way that I could cherish them and yet hold them lightly, in case I was wrong. That left me with a diverse blend of beliefs that agreed completely with no one. I could embrace the importance of a literal Incarnation—God becoming human in Christ—while also appreciating its profound metaphorical value even if it didn't happen. I realized that we can hold the Bible as divinely inspired *and still* accept it as what Marcus Borg calls it: a book written by humans about God.[3] I supported our local church's warm welcome to gays and lesbians while worrying that we didn't talk about God very much.

In short, I learned more about myself, more about what I could believe, and perhaps even a tiny bit more about God. I could use that exploration to feed my life in God. On the downside, the process left me feeling very much alone: there was no one to whom I could reveal *all* my ideas without subjecting myself to scorn.

The effect on our priest, however, was just the opposite. Early on, I expressed a desire not to let our discussions get in the way of his parish work, and his response stunned me: "If only you knew how deeply many clergy, myself included, long for discussions of this kind." No matter how strident we became with each other, he continued to echo that enthusiasm for dialogue—and even expressed regret when, for various reasons, it lapsed from time to time.

So clergy have precious few people with whom to discuss the things that move them. Yet I think the lesson goes further than that. Maybe, just maybe, dialogue can be a tonic for the gnawing loneliness that is part and parcel of the human condition. "What we know of other people is only our memory of the moments during which we knew them," wrote T. S. Eliot,[4] and we would prefer to avoid the truth that follows from this: no one can thoroughly know the soul of another. Yet there are ways to get close, and dialogue is one of the best. Even if we solve nothing, even if we end up learning nothing, we have talked. We have listened to others share the things that matter to them. Sometimes that simple connection is all we can ask—and more than we could ever hope for.

A Friend Indeed?

> Even my bosom friend in whom I trusted, who ate of
> my bread, has lifted the heel against me.
>
> (PSALM 41:9)

We don't think of friendships as causing pain. If they do, the thinking goes, they cease to be friendships. A recent experience in my life—born of a long-running dialogue—has convinced me otherwise.

I was delighted to see the e-mail from my old friend. She was perhaps my closest comrade in high school, when I was a strident fundamentalist and she a chain-smoking wisecracker. Differences aside, something enabled us to share our deepest thoughts with each other. At commencement, the good-bye hug from her brought me to tears.

Nearly thirty-five years later, I could still sense the closeness, but some things had changed. After an extremely difficult period in her twenties, she became a committed Christian—specifically, an evangelical who drew nourishment from the Trinity Broadcasting Network and Joyce Meyer and similar folks. I had moved to a different place in my faith, with a good deal of wildly progressive mixed in with some traditional beliefs.

After the initial reintroduction, she became a devoted and highly critical reader of my blogs, with an emphasis on *critical*. When I pondered a way forward on immigration, she slammed me for "not having a dog in this hunt." On other occasions, she pointed out instances of sloppy, superficial thinking. As a debate enthusiast, she pulled no punches and used no euphemisms. I wrote back with half-baked, barely civil answers and felt vaguely ridiculous. This correspondence hit so many raw nerves: my inability to express anger, my need for approval, a legacy of guilt from my fundamentalist past (because I had strayed from the One True Faith). At times I took comfort in the three thousand miles that separated us: she on the West Coast, I on the East.

In between these exchanges, we found our way to sharing about our lives. She was living right around the poverty line and had been for a long time. Her father had recently passed away, and the details of his estate absorbed a lot of her energy. She was at sea about the next phase of her life. Meanwhile, the process of discerning what I perceived as a call to write left me beset with doubts and anxiety. We were both, in short, vulnerable. For me at least, it was not the best time for sharp words and difficult debates.

At one point, I shared some of my thoughts on the nature of God—thoughts that are speculative, half-formed, and very close to my heart. When she ridiculed them, I reached the breaking point. I wrote back with as much anger as I could muster. This friendship had meant the world to me so long ago. Now, however, it was over.

This clearly was not the ideal dialogue. In fact, it barely fits the description we examined in chapter 1. Somewhere along the line, though, without my noticing it, these e-mail exchanges began to bear fruit. Most notably, my writing became better, more grounded, more thorough. Where before I had double-checked my facts, now I dug even deeper to understand the nuance behind them. I took extra care to think through the implications of my ideas. My friend's comment about "not having a dog in this hunt" opened my eyes to the inestimable value of personal experience in every discussion. (That, in turn, led to the reflections on the "arrogance of the abstract" in chapter 9.)

I wasn't the only one who benefited. My friend's e-mails were long, often circuitous, mostly stream of consciousness. At one point, she told me that those e-mails were, in effect, a journal—a place for her to explore situations in her life and think out loud about God's call for her. Perhaps she could have done all this in a private diary. Something about my continued attention to her writing, however, facilitated the process, and it was important to her.

We didn't correspond for several months. Then, slowly, my friend shared a Facebook post or two. We exchanged a few newsy and uncontroversial e-mails. Gradually, we fell back into conversation, with me more aware of the good that this difficult dialogue was having.

Eventually, the tone changed dramatically, and our lives did as well. After a long process of discernment and reflection, she applied to law school and was accepted on full scholarship. She is returning to the East Coast, where she grew up and feels most at home. In our recent correspondence, she has attributed her combative stance to the turmoil she was experiencing at the time. As for me, the doubts have passed; the call to write has emerged with far greater clarity, and it has brought me a serenity that I have never known before. The improvements in my writing have proved lasting.

Clearly, our dialogue of several years did not effect all these transformations. But it played a role in moving our individual lives forward, more deeply into the respective vocations that God has for us.

Not every dialogue is sustainable, and not every relationship is salvageable. Sometimes, in these situations, I have to walk away for a time to let tempers cool and my emotional wounds heal. At other times, we have no choice but to give up entirely.

Outside of dangerous or violent circumstances, however, we can make a good case for hanging in there when the dialogue turns difficult. The chances of our seeing eye-to-eye in these situations are remote. Yet sometimes, perseverance in dialogue can spark unexpected (and satisfying) resolutions. Often, it can provide a balm for loneliness, help people work out the circumstances of their lives, and make us better people. Notably, it expresses and echoes the faithfulness of God—offering compassion and empathy and welcome support to those whom we engage.

FOR YOUR CONSIDERATION ...

1. Search your memory for a discussion that went awry. Why did it fail? What good things came out of it?

2. Consider one of the polarizing issues of our times: gay marriage, for instance, or war, or capital punishment. What are the shopworn arguments that characterize each side? How might we reframe the issue to foster dialogue?

3. Come back to the issue about which you are wildly passionate and the people with whom you disagree (which you defined in response to the "For Your Consideration" questions from chapter 7). What kinds of policy initiatives or volunteer activities could you take up together that might allow you to see one another's humanity?

4. Did you learn other lessons from the sample dialogues we explored in this chapter—lessons that did not come up earlier in the book? What kind of lessons?

5. With what in this chapter do you disagree? Why?

Dialogue in the War Zone

The dialogues and relationships described in chapter 8 were a challenge, to be sure. At certain points we could have easily walked away from each other. But in the end, all of them worked out well and bore much fruit. It helped greatly that each dialogue included only two people who, by and large, were inclined to hang in there and make it work.

Some situations are not nearly so blessed—particularly when the conversation involves the flashpoints that have sparked hostility, hatred, and violence in the U.S. public square for decades. Some of these issues have drawn Christians into direct conflict, not only with people outside the Christian tradition, but with one another. All too often, a shared faith does nothing to calm the furious rhetoric and chronic antagonism.

And yet, even with these issues, small groups of people have done the unthinkable: convening with people on the "other side" to share their stories, foster bonds of affection, and begin to explore the most difficult issues. These groups have not come to grand resolutions. They *have* done something extraordinary. In this chapter we'll look at two of these dialogues and then consider a new, dialogic approach to a third flashpoint that often alienates Christians from their neighbors.

Abortion: Two Camps, One Room[1]

Any dialogue on abortion is difficult in the extreme. Imagine trying to start one between *leaders* of the pro-choice and pro-life movements.[2]

On the second to last day of 1994, a gunman walked into two women's health clinics near Boston and opened fire, killing two people and wounding five. Leaders on both sides of the debate condemned the shootings. Two of the most powerful officials in Massachusetts—William F. Weld, the governor, and Cardinal Bernard F. Law, the archbishop of Boston—called for a dialogue between the two sides.

Many civic leaders call for such things in the wake of tragedy, and rightly so. In this case, however, the Public Conversations Project (PCP) took them up on it.

PCP's history had positioned it for the task. Five years before, a televised debate—which, like too many of our televised debates, had turned angry and confrontational—deeply disturbed family therapist Laura Chasin, and she began to wonder if the counseling strategies from her field might help create authentic dialogue on issues in the public square. Together with a handful of colleagues, she founded PCP to make it happen. Abortion drew their attention from the beginning: through a series of eighteen dialogues with more than one hundred participants, Chasin and her colleagues developed a reliable model of opening new ways for pro-choice and pro-life adherents to communicate with one another.

They would need it for the challenge that faced them in the wake of the shootings. After consulting widely with community leaders, PCP invited a group of six remarkable women to meet together. Their differences could hardly be starker: they included the president and a former board member from the Planned Parenthood League of Massachusetts, the executive director of Mass NARAL (the state affiliate of the National Abortion and Reproductive Rights Action League), a consultant for the

Pro-Life Committee of the National Conference of Catholic Bishops, a past president of Massachusetts Citizens for Life, and the director of the Pro-Life Office of the Archdiocese of Boston.

Three pro-choice, three pro-life, dialoguing under the strictest confidence to protect their safety and avoid muddying the discussion with input from outside groups. The plan was for four meetings over one month.

They met for 5½ years.

At the start, everyone was beset with anxieties—including the two facilitators, Chasin and Susan Podziba, a public policy mediator who operates Susan Podziba & Associates. From the start, the participants sparred over language, including the terms *pro-choice* and *pro-life* and the name for what developed over nine months in a woman's womb. They found it excruciating to honor their commitments *not* to argue for their cause.

Two elements of this dialogue, among others, contributed substantially to its success. One involved the purpose, or rather what the purpose was *not*: an attempt to change one another's minds, compromise, or even forge common ground. The objectives were both simpler and deeper than that: to truly understand one another, build relationships of mutual respect, find a way around the typical rhetoric, clarify differences and shared values, and reduce the risk of violence.

The other element involved the strategies and ground rules that PCP brought to the table (or forged with the participants). In addition to seeking out language acceptable to all, the participants agreed to speak only for themselves (not for their agencies) and to avoid interrupting or making personal attacks. They created a list of "hot buttons" to work around. They discussed stereotypes that each held concerning the people on the other side. They explored various aspects of abortion. They told their personal stories.

Slowly, they began to understand one another. Most important, they hung in there.

Those 5½ years created something of a miracle. As you might expect, all the pro-choice dialogue participants attended a service to mark the one-year anniversary of the clinic shootings—but so did two of the pro-life participants. When a pro-life group from Virginia announced a trip to Massachusetts to celebrate the shootings, the three pro-life participants in the dialogue wrote to the leader distancing themselves from him and dissuading him from coming. The participants' public statements on abortion took on a new, less divisive tone. As they wrote in their *Boston Sunday Globe* article of 2001, "[Now,] when we face our opponent, we see her dignity and goodness."

What can we take away from this extraordinary dialogue? Surely, it carries many lessons about goal setting, the value of the PCP model, and other areas. For me, however, the most compelling lessons are also the most blindingly obvious:

1. Dialogue can work in extreme circumstances—even when the issue has driven people to violence, even with the scars inflicted by decades of hatred and rhetoric, even when people can barely agree on the very language they use. Careful, thoughtful facilitation makes a huge difference, but it needs the support of good intentions and deep commitment on the part of the participants. Dialogue as a habit of the heart has a major role to play here: its basic orientation toward openness, listening, and seeing the other as human makes good intentions and deep commitment the default position in the core of our being.

2. Dialogue takes time—lots of it—and the results are often intangible. The participants in this dialogue spent more than 150 hours together over 5½ years. As we have seen, their efforts made a difference: partly in the way they engaged the world, partly by ratcheting down the inflammatory rhetoric (for a while at least) in one major U.S. city. Critics might question the return on such an investment of time and energy. But this question assumes that results are the whole point. As people of faith, we march to a different beat: we are called, first and foremost, not to results but to *faithfulness*. By participating in dialogue, we are faithfully fulfilling God's call to be peacemakers, to be people of "patience, kindness, generosity, faithfulness, gentleness, and self-control"

(Galatians 5:22–23). By expending so much effort in the process, we are incarnating the basic truth that we live our lives not for ourselves, but for something much larger, which allows us to focus our energy where it is needed. Spending 5½ years in one dialogue with six people to create a small but profound difference in one corner of the world: that effort echoes the God who would become incarnate in a tiny backwater of the Roman Empire, delivering the divine message—and dying—in utter obscurity. Ultimately, his life and death became something so much larger than anyone could have imagined. Who knows whether our own dialogues in our own small corners of the world might have a similar impact?

The LGBTQ Firestorm: From Anxiety to Wonder

It wasn't the big-city traffic that had my nerve endings on edge. It was the destination: a haphazardly convened band of twelve strangers—evangelical Christians of various stripes—who were gathering for two intense days to have a "gay Christian dialogue."

Many, many people would consider that term an oxymoron, and with good reason: few issues have riven the Church in the past thirty years quite like sexual orientation. Our denominations have endured tumultuous synods, sessions, diocesan conventions, church meetings, one after another after another. Attempts at authentic dialogue have often degenerated into simple restatements of position, power struggles, and epithets like *abomination* and *homophobia* that create more heat than light. In my conversations with people affected by this issue, I hear a bone weariness—accompanied at times by the resigned wish that the issue would just "go away."

While connected with this larger landscape, however, my anxiety sprang from more personal issues. For one, I had lived on both sides of the spectrum characterized by this issue—in my youth as a conservative Christian, now as an eclectic mix that skews closer to the progressive end. I have a substantial stake in my current beliefs about LGBTQ issues. Now here comes this gathering that, by definition, would call us to be open to the other. What if I had to change my mind? What if I heard something that forced me back into the stance that (as some denominational formulations put it) "homosexual practice is incompatible with scripture"?

The other issue was even more personal: the fact that, in terms of this topic, I don't fit a neat category. I am a monogamous, heterosexual man with a vibrant feminine side that occasionally borders on girly. I've spent more than twenty years working this out, and the work continues. I love who I am and am terrified to proclaim it too freely. How much of me could I really share with this group of people?

As it turned out, I was able to share a lot of myself. And my beliefs did change—but not in the way I expected.

During the two days, we engaged in the types of exercises common to many such gatherings. On the first day, our convener posted sheets of paper around the room, each with one word on it, and asked us to write our reactions to that word on the papers. At another point, we pulled random slips of paper with statements about sexual orientation on them, then expressed our feelings about the statements. We painted, with general hilarity the result. There were exercises involving hula hoops.

Were we dancing around the issue? Not even close—because, as with the dialogue over abortion in Boston, direct theological debate was never the point. It is nearly automatic, when approaching a done-to-death conversation like this directly, to fall into the same tired arguments and stereotypes and simplistic assertions. So the objective here was to do something else. As one participant said, "We're here not to define, but to be present with one another with no expectations." Early on, the convener talked effusively about building a new community.

Most extraordinary by far, however, were the stories—because the people in the room absolutely defied simple description. In this group of twelve, I discovered gay and lesbian people who, while fully owning their orientation, have chosen celibacy because of a deep fealty to their faith tradition. I found people who believe that nearly all consensual sex is blessed and expresses aspects of God. I spent time with a gay man who, out of a deep and undeniable love, married his closest friend—of the opposite sex. I encountered people who identify as queer and those who believe that marriage should be between one man and one woman. In every last one of them, I encountered someone who was striving to live in obedience to the call of Christ.

From that remarkable diversity of perspectives, we plunged into issues and conversations that never arise in the shouting over sexual orientation. We bemoaned how rarely we experience physical touch in our society—despite how much and how deeply we crave it—because it has been so sexualized. We ruminated over the messiness of life, the notion that God is often found in that very messiness, and our longing for simplicity, especially simple answers to difficult questions. We talked about the craving for intimacy and belonging and how we could live that out as Christians. We wondered about separating out doctrinal necessities from cultural markers. We discussed how the Church could repent of the way it has historically treated differences—and how we could create a climate in which young people feel safe to speak up in church about sexual orientation.

Not everything was easy to hear. One person openly wondered why Christians find it so hard to talk about sex at all, and the tension in the room spiked. Another chafed at the whole idea of marriage equality as the dominant heterosexual community's attempt to impose its own relationship model on gay and lesbian people. Still another broke down in tears.

But our convener's words proved prophetic. We were there to build a community, and by the end we had done so. The sense of intimacy, of genuine respect and love for one another, was palpable. I am still in touch with several members of that group and cherish my bond with them.

Like the Boston dialogue, this experience didn't come close to "resolving the issue" on a grand level. It would be far too much to expect a two-day session to bring closure to a thirty-year crisis. But it did demonstrate dialogue's ability to create bonds across divides.

What else can we learn from this dialogue? I see at least three takeaways:

1. Dialogue *can* change our minds, and the change can surprise us. I worried that the session would push me back into
   a conservative stance. It actually did the opposite, moving
   me toward welcoming multiple forms of sexual expression
   while shifting my concern to more basic sexual values, like
   commitment, self-giving, and spiritual as well as physical
   intimacy.

2. Issues are more complex than we think—even if we already
   think they're complex. Coming into the session, I thought I
   had a basic handle on the topic. I never imagined the kaleidoscope of ways in which people actually lived around it. And
   I'd given short shrift to the endless nuances and contradic-
   tions and meta-issues that this one issue raises. It may seem
   obvious after the fact—of *course* our need for physical touch
   has a bearing on our sexuality; of *course* this is not just about
   sex, but about loving relationships—but these things often
   elude us. And exploring them is not, as some might think, a
   way to "muddy the waters" or "dance around the truth"; in
   most cases, at least, it is an honest attempt to see the issue
   from every perspective, so we can validate, revise, or overhaul
   our thinking in closer alignment with reality. Our mind-sets
   from chapter 5, especially *I don't know,* can help us to hold
   our minds open as we encounter the complexity of the issue
   at hand.

The third point is akin to the second:

3. Beware the arrogance of the abstract. When our beloved church
   elder came out more than thirty years ago, my first instinct was
   to search scripture and pray and reflect over the issue. Nothing
   wrong with that. But afterward, I formed an opinion and basically *stayed there.* It never occurred to me that hearing the stories of people who wrestled with the issue would have any
   value. It was all about truth, and truth was in scripture, right?

   This, I think, goes back to our old way of thinking about
   the self: as separate aspects, each unaffected by the others. In

this case, the argument goes, only one part of us—our capacity to reason—is the "proper" part to engage in the discussion. We need to "think this through rationally," "take the emotions out of it," and so on. Now it *is* true that, in many cases, emotions get overheated and the people involved can best move forward by returning to a place of calm. But by removing emotions, spiritual reflections, even physical responses to an issue, we may remove other ways of apprehending truth, and thus our discussion of the issue will be far more limited—and arid—than if we approached the issue holistically, using all our faculties.

Sticking to the abstract, then, excludes potentially valuable aspects of ourselves from the dialogue. It also excludes the potentially valuable wisdom of others. Some insights into the truth of an issue can only come from people who have lived it. This is why, for instance, many people react with anger when a group of male decision makers—legislators, archbishops, what have you—debate contraception policy. They do not have access to the truth one learns by living with the policy day by day. As one participant in our "gay Christian dialogue" said during our time together, "When people tell their stories, new depths open up."

After church one Sunday, a longtime member of our parish walked up to me. He had read about a resolution to be considered at our upcoming diocesan convention, and he knew I was a delegate with voting power. In most contexts, he is a calm, steady-as-she-goes fellow with great intelligence and a wicked sense of humor. Not that day. He asked me to vote against the resolution—it could have been read as having a negative effect on LGBTQ people, and my friend is gay—and when I probed his position further, his eyes flashed with anger and pain. In that single look I saw more truth about the issue than I could have seen any other way: the deep impact of a rather arcane resolution on the lives of people.

Without question, the abstract has a major role to play. It helps us make sense of the world's messiness. It opens doors to communicating in a common language, with ideas we can understand. It takes us out of the realm of the purely subjective. But when we approach issues from the abstract alone, we do so at our peril—and the peril of others.

Evangelism: Making Disciples of All Nations

Does the heading to this section make you cringe? You're not alone. "Spreading the Gospel" with any method more assertive than "living the Gospel" runs afoul of my deepest-seated sensitivities. For years I have attempted to tune out sermons on the topic, picking up small shards of guilt with each one.

Unfortunately, small shards accumulate. While they didn't precipitate an emotional crisis, they were enough of a drag on my well-being to inspire some soul searching. As with the "gay Christian dialogue" just described, that soul searching introduced me to a way of thinking about evangelism that I didn't know existed.

Sermons on evangelism pop up in more churches than you might think. People often associate the word with evangelical or conservative churches, which focus on "reaching the world for Christ" and "fulfilling the Great Commission." In mainstream churches, the language may be different— they tend to talk about church growth and hold "Bring a Friend Sundays"— but the message is the same. Reach out. Tell your neighbor. Share your faith.

It's not that easy anymore—if it ever was.

Evangelism in any guise—evangelical or progressive—puts postmodern Christians in a delicate position. On the one hand, we live with a call to spread the good news of God's reign, however we might interpret that call. On the other, we live in the shadow of Christendom's history, which has given attempts to spread the good news a very bad name. On the third (yes, we need three hands for this), we live in a skeptical, pluralistic world with an astonishingly short attention span. If people outside the Christian tradition aren't hostile to evangelism because of its history, they are indifferent to the message because it appears to hold little relevance to their lives right now.

Under these conditions, it's reasonable to ask some hard questions. Is there a better way to look at this thing called evangelism? Is there a *dialogic* way to look at evangelism: a way that allows us to share our lives generously with others—including, but not limited to, our faith—while honoring the listener and bridging divides? To answer that question, let's look at our three "hands" one at a time.

First, the call to evangelize. Many strands of the Church have interpreted Jesus's words at the end of Matthew's Gospel (Matthew 28:18–20) as a call to all Christians. According to this interpretation, we are to "make disciples of all nations, baptizing them in the name of the Father and of the Son and of the Holy Spirit, and teaching them to obey everything that I have commanded you." Granted, our approach to this call may differ. Evangelicals see it as helping others make a personal commitment to Christ; progressives may regard it as bringing others to church or sharing the *message* that Christ preached. Whatever the specifics, it is still tempting for progressive Christians to discount the whole practice. Isn't it essentially judgmental? Why not just "live and let live"? Why, if people are living good lives and following their own brand of faith, would it make sense for us to "force our religion down their throats"?

That question brings us right into the second "hand": a negative, even hostile, perception of evangelism. In many ways, Christendom has brought that perception on itself. All too often throughout history, from the horrors of the Crusades to forced conversions on the mission field, "spreading the Gospel" has been intricately associated with coercion, intimidation, and violence. More recently, the sermons of some revivalist preachers and televangelists have been noted primarily for their condemnation of specific groups, or their dire warnings of hell, instead of a proclamation of love, peacemaking, and other fruits of the Spirit. The disrespect shown by some Christians toward other faith traditions has outraged the adherents of those faith traditions. It's no wonder that an old high school friend of mine would not even let me mention Jesus when I visited her shortly after graduation. She is not alone in her hostility.

Many people, however, are not hostile toward evangelism; rather, they ignore it entirely. The dynamics of postmodern culture (our third "hand" for necessitating a rethink of evangelism) loom large here. For one thing, as consumers, we're exposed to hundreds of messages every day. To function in that kind of media frenzy, we develop an ability to sort and (mostly) reject these messages at the blink of an eye. Is it relevant to me, right here, right now? Is it easy to grasp quickly? If the answer is no, the message gets dismissed, because we have to move on to the next thing. It is not easy for most people to grasp the relevance of a two-thousand-year-old itinerant Jewish rabbi to a life of tablet computing and nanotechnology.

This quick-sorting ability goes hand in hand with our culture's pervasive skepticism. People who have grown up with the Internet, especially, excel at sniffing out sales messages and the vested interests behind them. The first false note turns them right off. This is one reason why ads and TV commercials often say so little about the products they're selling: their objective is to engage the audience (through humor, poignancy, or whatever emotion makes sense) and thus get past the instant objection to the sales pitch.

Moreover, why would postmodern people listen to a specific religious claim in a free, individualistic society, where all people are entitled to their beliefs and all beliefs are perceived as equally valid? Traditional evangelism—at least the versions that claim Christ as the only way to God—cannot help but fall short.

So why are we having this conversation? Why not just dismiss evangelism entirely? Because—despite the checkered history of the practice and the rampant cultural skepticism—there are compelling reasons for sharing our faith. The Jesus of Christianity speaks a message of peacemaking to a world at war, a passion for justice to a world that has rarely experienced it. He speaks of love and self-sacrifice for something larger than ourselves, of inner transformation and change for the better. Moreover, the inner connection with the God of Jesus, a connection we foster through the practices described in chapter 4, brings us more than an orientation toward dialogue. It also brings us joy, healing, strength of character, and other virtues. And these benefits are for everyone. So why would we refrain from sharing such good news?

Perhaps we *do* share, but in a completely different way. Maybe we join the conversation. Maybe we *dialogue*.

The implications of evangelism-as-dialogue are profound—and they will not surprise you if you've read this far. By joining the conversation, we foster relationships, not as a pretext to deliver a message, but to share the lives and hopes and fears and disappointments of those we befriend.

In doing so, we show what we profess in our faith: the love of others and commitment to relationship that Christ preached.

This is especially true when we take evangelism-as-dialogue one step further and *just listen*. In listening—putting ourselves aside to hear, and reach, the other—our love reaches its fullest expression as *self-giving*. This self-giving brand of listening affirms the dignity of the other person and the value of her beliefs. Moreover, listening is a balm for the rampant loneliness that plagues so many of us. Why lead with words to communicate this extravagant love of God when silence expresses it so much more eloquently? Then, if and when we do speak, we speak from the heart of God's message—love—as those who have attempted to live it. In our skeptical society, people who back up their words with deeds become trusted sources. Living what we say is a powerful way to deliver the message of love.

Evangelism-as-dialogue also moves us toward a simple sharing of our experience of God and away from a focus on "results." The results orientation puts considerable pressure on us to "close the deal": to get evangelized people to take the next step, however we might conceive it. Faced with that pressure, we may either lean into the aggressive, alienating brand of evangelism or, more likely, simply avoid the whole affair. But again, as we noted in the discussion of the abortion dialogue, why focus on results anyway? Even conservative believers, who see the result in the direst terms—a matter of heaven or hell—also believe that the results are solely up to God. Evangelism-as-dialogue places our emphasis where it belongs: on our own actions, on our own faithfulness in following God wherever God may take us.

I've had the privilege of dialoguing with people from all sorts of belief systems. These dialogues often bear fruit in two ways. People who think that all Christians fit a narrow stereotype—particularly a stereotype of uncompromising rigidity—come away realizing that it ain't necessarily so. Maybe, as a result, they become just a little more receptive to Christianity. Meanwhile, by hearing their perspectives, I learn to appreciate the thought behind them and see how they might illuminate unexplored aspects of my own faith.

Just as important, each of us comes face-to-face with the human being behind the "opposing" belief system. That cannot help but foster compassion and peace.

FOR YOUR CONSIDERATION ...

1. Consider the other side of a topic discussed in this chapter: abortion, LGBTQ issues, or evangelism. Without judging, see if you can fathom the line of reasoning behind it. Seek out a website that attempts to lay out the position in a civil manner (ProCon.org is an excellent place to start). What do you hear in this position? Can you see how a reasonable, goodhearted person *might* come to that belief? How might you open a dialogue with such a person?

2. What other topics would you consider "war zones"—conflicts that have raged with seemingly no hope of dialogue? How would you start a dialogue on these topics?

3. With what in this chapter do you disagree? Why?

A Gentle Challenge to Our Culture

W e don't talk much about *counterculture* anymore. The word conjures up the 1960s with its echoes of revolution and antiwar demonstrations and flower power. Perhaps you never thought you'd be part of anything that could be labeled countercultural.

Well, now you are.

In sociology, the word has a more precise definition: "cultural patterns that strongly oppose those widely accepted in a society," as one text puts it.[1] By that definition, dialogue as a habit of the heart is countercultural on several levels. We have already seen one of them in abundance: Intractable conflict has become a cultural norm in many spheres of activity. We have come to expect it as standard operating procedure from elected officials and pundits. In so many church controversies, school board fights, and relationship squabbles, the possibility of dialogue as an option never crosses our minds. When it does, we worry that any attempt to reach across divides will somehow compromise our principles. Dialogue flies in the face of all this intractability: its very first instinct is to listen, to seek peace, to try to understand. It approaches from a position of openness rather than defensiveness. It does not seek to interrupt the other or even formulate a response while the other is speaking. Some people may see this not only as countercultural, but as dangerous; they have built their careers, even their whole orientation toward life, on conflict, so an orientation toward dialogue leaves them adrift.

This sort of dynamic brings us to another way in which dialogue is countercultural: its resonance with the message of Jesus. His emphasis on mercy over rigid observance of the law—healing on the Sabbath, talking with women of a despised class or ethnicity, dining with the dreaded tax collectors and even calling one of them to be an apostle— ran him afoul of the authorities. When called to task by these same authorities, Jesus challenged them to reflect and reconsider their own assumptions. Dialogue presents a similar challenge to our long-held assumptions and rigid categories, no matter how gently or delicately we pursue it. Many people deride dialogue as an attempt to "just all get along," as "fuzzy thinking" for the sake of avoiding conflict. It is quite the opposite. But rather than take up our adversarial culture's typical approach to challenge—shout, defend, cut off conversation—it seeks to engage the other in a deep experience of listening and conversing. It may not directly issue the challenge to change one's thinking, but that is often the effect.

There is also a third way in which dialogue is countercultural. It has to do with values that our culture prizes above many others: efficiency, speed, results, return on investment.

As we have seen, dialogue is a funny thing. Sometimes it succeeds beyond all expectation, the parties reach consensus, and everyone moves forward together. Sometimes it fails, we end up squabbling, and the answer arises from the ashes. Often it falls short of uncovering the truth, but satisfies the deepest longings of our souls, like the hunger for companionship or the need to be heard. At times it fails to achieve a policy solution, but moves the participants to see the legitimacy of the "other side" and the humanity of its advocates. Sometimes dialogue sheds little light on a situation but somehow, mysteriously, brings us closer.

Maybe, just maybe, we can say that dialogue *never* fails. Often it just succeeds in unexpected ways, and we fail to perceive it.

Now consider what this book asks of us. It asks us to take up a different orientation of the heart through a different way of life. It requires a highly intentional practice of spirituality and "practical living." It can spark phenomenal transformation in us. We're supposed to do all this for a result that may or may not happen—or, more precisely, may or may not align with our definition of success. That's not what we do as postmodern people: we plan, build strategies, specify results, and then execute the strategies to achieve those results. We carefully measure the return on our investment of time, energy, relationships, and money.

The point here is not to malign the envisioning of goals or the development of strategies. Goal orientation is a good thing in many instances; it's difficult to get where we need to go if we don't know where that is. The problem comes when achievement of the goal—expressed in tangible, measurable, short-term results—becomes the only measure of success or failure. By that standard, the cultivation of dialogue as a habit of the heart is wasteful in the extreme. It requires so much effort for a return that is anything but certain, and rarely measurable.

This sort of "poor return on investment" will sound familiar to anyone who consciously pursues the spiritual life. As we open ourselves to God, we find ourselves redefining success and failure. The roadblocks we suddenly encounter begin to look like opportunities, placed in our way to rearrange our thinking and redirect our path. As we see the outcome, our confidence in God grows, and we come to trust the sudden obstacles and the switchbacks and the best-laid plans turned to rubble. We understand St. Paul when he writes that "all things work together for good for those who love God" (Romans 8:28).

Another funny thing happens as we move forward in the spiritual life: our time horizon grows longer. The more we come to understand our place in the universe—as one contributor among many to the good of the world—the less we worry about "getting it done" as opposed to just doing what we can, whatever that may be. We can plant "seeds" here and there and let them take root, or not, in their own sweet time. Striving for results becomes less important than doing the right thing and leaving the results to God.

What does all this mean for dialogue? Simply that we can never know the full effect of the dialogues we engage in. That makes every dialogue worth the effort, no matter how fruitless it may seem at the beginning, no matter how frustrating it becomes when it stalls, no matter how disillusioning it is when everything seems to come apart. Our calling is not so much to achieve success as to keep talking and listening and loving one another.

Anything can happen when we start to talk. Nothing will happen if we don't. That alone makes the way of dialogue a journey worth taking.

∞ ACKNOWLEDGMENTS

I can't tell you how many times I have scanned acknowledgments and run across a phrase like this: "Writing a book is not a one-person task. Indeed, this book could not have happened without the input of many people." I always figured authors made that statement as a lovely courtesy that bore no truth whatsoever.

Boy, was I wrong.

Over the past few years, I have seen countless examples of how this book would have been so much poorer without this edit from x or that piece of advice from y or the introduction to a spiritual practice from z. Some of these wise and generous people have been enjoying their heavenly reward for five hundred years; others are among my closest relatives. I am sure the following list will miss some of these folks, and for that I apologize. My deepest gratitude goes to them and to the following:

- The monks of Holy Cross Monastery and its sister houses—particularly my spiritual director, Brother Ronald Haynes—for providing the place and the insight for me to learn, and fall in love with, many of the spiritual practices in this book.

- My friends in the local chapter of the Thomas Merton Society, whose Tuesday night Office and silent prayer have taught me the joys of *these* practices.

- My sister Ingrid, the best of spiritual friends, who convinced me to write what I know for the people I know.

- My daughter, Whitney, for many helpful suggestions, including the nudge to put many more anecdotes in the book.

- My good friend Mary Egan, a source of constant encouragement and cheerleading.

- My colleagues at The Kaleel Jamison Consulting Group, Inc.—particularly Judith Katz and Fred Miller, whose pioneering ideas I hear echoed throughout this book, and Corey Jamison, who has insisted I complete this project and has given me the space to do so.

- The people whose stories appear in this book, for their willingness to share those stories and walk alongside me through sometimes difficult dialogues.

- My brother-in-law Mike Weber, whose advice led me to rewrite the fable of the blind men and the elephant.

- St. Thérèse of Lisieux, whose spirituality has shaped me more than any other holy person (Jesus excepted).

- Emily Wichland, my sharp-eyed and encouraging editor, and the other good people at SkyLight Paths Publishing.

- Sandy Heierbacher of the National Coalition for Dialogue & Deliberation, whose unsolicited tweet got me involved in a great organization and introduced me to the big wide world of dialogue.

- Bob Stains of the Public Conversations Project, for his constant enthusiasm and for being part of an organization that is truly making the world better.

- All those who took the time to read and comment on *Why Can't We Talk?*—including Kay Lindahl, who wrote a wonderful Foreword; our church's deacon, Nancy Rosenblum, who lent her wisdom to chapter 2; and the people whose quotes and kind words you will see elsewhere in this book.

Two others deserve particular attention in this space. The conversations with my sister-in-law Jane Weber have galvanized my interest in dialogue in a way that may never have happened otherwise. Her editorial remarks transformed not only key sections of the book, but also my entire attitude toward a particular group of people that I have learned to love all over again. Her example provides a lasting model of how to dialogue with generosity.

Then there is my wife, Prudence. Words fail me here. Her example of maturity and compassion is an inspiration to me. Her tireless patience with the demands of book authorship is a blessing I couldn't live without. Most of all, as she would say, she lets me be me. I could wish for no better partner.

Of course, all credit for this effort—and for everything else—must go to the true protagonist of this book: God. *Soli deo gloria.*

APPENDIX

Spiritual Practices for the Way of Dialogue

If you're a fan of brain teasers, you've undoubtedly run across this type of problem: *You are on a quest. To complete the quest, you must [name of task here], using only [list of seemingly random objects here].*

This appendix is like that brain teaser—only the objects are less random. Indeed, people of faith have used them for centuries to cultivate a deeper connection with God. They have a way of opening and softening the soul so that God can reshape its contents in alignment with the divine will. We have already seen how this work of God can open us to dialogue; it can also bring us an abundant life, filled with love, joy, and the exhilarating sense of living for something larger than oneself.

Typical of anything that is centuries-old, there are myriads of "how to" resources outlining specific steps and techniques for spiritual practices. This appendix makes no attempt to summarize them. Rather, each section gives you a simple starting point—often drawing on my personal experience with the practice—and lists a key resource or two to help you move deeper if you so choose.

As you ponder these practices, keep a few things in mind. Every practice aims essentially at one goal: deepening the encounter between you and God. Because you are unique, the way you approach your spiritual life will be unique, too. So feel free to adapt these practices, mix and match, or explore further for others that speak to your soul.

Even more important, these practices are *not* techniques for us to "work our way to God." Rather, they till the soil of our soul to make us more receptive to God's action in our lives. *Everything* depends on God's initiative. This knowledge relieves us of the "pressure to perform"—a more pervasive pressure than one might think!—and allows us to rest in the arms of God.

Moreover, because God interacts with us in innumerable ways, we never quite know how God has visited us at any given time. As a result, it's best *not* to assess whether today's centering prayer or yesterday's Bible reading was "productive" or "useful." Our fleeting emotions during these exercises—like comfort, ecstasy, or the lack thereof—give us little reliable indication of the movement of God. We may feel absolutely nothing while praying the psalms, for instance, and yet God may have done God's deepest work in our souls at precisely that time.

Over time, we often do develop a sense of divine movement in our souls. But in so many cases, all we can trust is that God is always there, always at work within us. And we *will* see the fruit of our cooperation in the process. (It *is* possible, however, to pursue a particular spiritual practice for months and never have it produce fruit in your life. In cases like that, it's worth considering whether another spiritual practice might work better for you.)

Silent Prayer

For all the words that have been written about silent prayer, I believe our French worshiper from chapter 4 has captured its very essence: "I look at him, he looks at me." By holding that simple essence in our minds, we can avoid getting overly fussy about the details of this or that technique.

Not that these techniques are irrelevant. Quite the contrary: various forms of silent prayer have opened millions of souls to the presence of God. And it helps to start with a process of some sort. So here are some basic steps for silent prayer:

1. Find a quiet space you can visit easily—somewhere in or close to your home.

2. Be seated in a comfortable position: on the floor or in a chair; legs crossed or uncrossed; feet on the floor or elevated; eyes closed or open.

3. Breathe deeply and slowly. Let your mind go blank.

4. Once your mind is calm and your breathing settled, gradually turn your attention to God. Focus on God for the remainder of your prayer time.

5. At the end of the time, take several deep breaths, get up slowly, and go about your day.

It can be that simple—and that difficult. Right from the beginning, questions and obstacles arise:

- *Let my mind go blank? Are you kidding?* Yes, it *is* a lot to ask amid today's packed schedules and constant input. To counteract this, many people focus on their breath, devoting all their conscious attention to the slow inhale and exhale. Others keep their eyes open, choose a spot on the wall or in the sky, and focus on that. This sustained attention gently draws our minds away from the mental clutter.

- *What does it mean to "focus on God"?* We *can* simply sit and wait in expectation for the presence of God. Here, too, however, techniques can help. Many people focus on a mantra—a word like *God, Jesus,* or *love.* Others gaze steadily at an icon or cross. Praying the rosary, with its repetition of the Hail Mary, is good for focusing the mind. Still others will take a verse from scripture into their prayer time. Somehow, as our conscious attention dwells on whatever focal point we've chosen, it frees the rest of our brains—perhaps our souls?—to commune with God.

- *How long?* As with physical exercise, it helps to start slowly—say, five minutes at first—and work your way up. Our regular prayer group prays silently for thirty minutes, and I love that time span. Your experience may be different.

- *My attention wanders constantly.* You would not believe how many thinkers and sages have written about this—and how many words they have devoted to it. Keep this in mind: *distractions are normal.* They happen to everyone, all the time. The trick is not to fight them or feel guilty about them, but simply to note their presence, even chuckle at them a bit ("Ha! There goes my brain again!"), and return your attention gently to God.

- *OK, I've tried this a couple of times, and it didn't work.* As with physical exercise, it takes a while to become comfortable with the practice and let it do its work. The more you pray over time, the more natural it becomes, and the less you can imagine your life without it.

No discussion of silent prayer would be complete without mentioning the work of Fathers William Meninger, Basil Pennington, and Thomas Keating. These three Trappist monks have been central to the modern description and practice of *centering prayer,* a technique with its origins in medieval Christian mysticism. Some of the steps above draw on their work. You can read about centering prayer at www.centeringprayer.com or in *Finding Grace at the Center: The Beginning of Centering Prayer* by Basil Pennington, Thomas Keating, and Thomas E. Clarke.

Praying the Psalms

In one sense, praying the psalms almost needs no explanation. It is easy enough to open your Bible, start with Psalm 1, read maybe three psalms to God—then pick up with Psalm 4 the next day and do it all over again. This is a perfectly legitimate approach.

Still, there is great value in praying the Daily Office: the cycle of prescribed psalms, readings, and prayers said at specific times of the day. Monastic residents gather to say the Office several times a day (typically anywhere from four to nine times, depending on the monastery), praying through all 150 psalms in a week, a month, or another designated time span. Those of us who live outside monasteries can adapt the frequency of the Office to our own needs (see the Rule of Life section below).

But why use the Daily Office? For one thing, it gives users a systematic immersion in the rich words of scripture. "Praying using the Daily

Office adds a dimension of discipline and order to our prayers," writes Mark Buetow, former pastor of Gloria Dei Lutheran Church in New Orleans. "It fills our ears with God's Word and puts that Word back upon our lips as prayer."[1] Moreover, the combination of texts on any given day reflects the (inspired?) wisdom of the people who composed and organized them in this way. The resulting juxtapositions often spark fascinating insights: a verse from Psalm 3, for instance, might illuminate a reading from the Letter of James in a way that had never occurred to you before.

If you opt for the Daily Office, consider:

- *Purchasing a breviary,* a book with the forms and texts for the Daily Office. Catholic breviaries come in several versions, varying in length from the aptly named *Shorter Christian Prayer* to the four-volume *Liturgy of the Hours*—which includes, among other things, liturgies to honor individual saints. The Episcopal/ Anglican *Book of Common Prayer* includes not only the forms of the Daily Office but also the Eucharist (the principal form of Sunday worship), liturgies for special occasions, the psalms, and other useful texts. Monasteries and monastic orders often publish their own breviaries. If you are a member of a specific denomination, check to see if it offers a breviary of its own. One practical benefit of breviaries is that they are convenient: all the words you will need for a given Office in a single book (or set of books).

- *Using a lectionary*—a schedule of regular scripture readings throughout the year. This aligns our prayer and readings with wide swaths of the Church, so you are connecting with the Christian community beyond yourself even when you're praying alone. As mentioned in chapter 4, a lectionary also prevents us from praying only the psalms and passages we like; the encounter with a frame of mind outside ourselves tends to bring unexpected insight and make us larger of spirit. The Catholic Church has its own lectionary; most Protestant denominations use the Revised Common Lectionary (see the Vanderbilt University site, http://lectionary.library.vanderbilt.edu/).

- *Taking your time.* It's better to pray one psalm at a reflective pace than five in a rush. Some psalters (books of the psalms) place an asterisk halfway through the verse; it's a good place to pause briefly and let the first half of the verse sink in. This practice also slows you down automatically.

Absorbing the Scriptures

One Episcopal prayer perfectly captures an invaluable way to read the Bible and apply it to our lives: we are to "read, mark, learn, and inwardly digest." Some of the tips in the previous section apply here: follow the lectionary, take your time.

One popular method of scriptural study is *lectio divina* (Latin for "divine reading"): a slow, reflective reading whose purpose is not exegesis or scholarship but connecting our hearts with God's heart through the wisdom of the words. The *Lectio Divina* website (www.lectio-divina.org) is an excellent place to learn about this ancient practice; so are many others available via online search. Another fine source is Christine Valters Paintner's *Lectio Divina—the Sacred Art: Transforming Words and Images into Heart-Centered Prayer*. Here is how I practice *lectio:*

- Because I pray Morning Prayer from *The Book of Common Prayer*—complete with readings from the lectionary in the back—my *lectio* focuses on a book of the Bible that balances out what I pray in the morning. So, if I am reading the Gospel of Matthew in Morning Prayer, I might choose the book of Ecclesiastes for *lectio.* If I'm deep into Exodus in the morning, I might focus on one of Paul's letters during my divine reading. Whatever the book, I read it straight through, one passage at a time.

- As I read the passage through the first time—slowly!—I pay attention to anything that catches my attention or generates a response within me.

- After the first time through, I go back to what caught my attention and dwell on that. It might be a word, a phrase, an unusual reaction from someone in the passage, even a thought of "how that person must have felt, hearing that under these conditions."

Rather than analyze this, I savor it, turning it over in my mind and heart. Sometimes this savoring uncovers other thoughts, and I spend time with those, too.

- Eventually, my focus on the reading turns subtly toward a focus on God. I talk with God (verbally or silently) about some aspect of the reading and how it touches me; then I spend a few moments in silent prayer. I close the book and move on.

A few extra ideas:

- Short is good with *lectio*. Stick to an individual incident or parable, maybe a dozen proverbs, or what have you. Otherwise, you might be overwhelmed with a myriad of insights. However …

- In some of the historical or prophetic books, little might emerge over a long passage. In these cases, I tend to read until an overall insight comes together or I reach a convenient stopping point.

- I include books outside the Bible in my *lectio* as well, varying the book I use from session to session. These other books might include writings of the saints or well-respected spiritual authors, as well as the sacred books of other faith traditions. My choice of book on any given day depends on what may feed my soul that day. My internal compass tends to be a reliable guide.

Rule of Life

A Rule of Life outlines the values, principles, and practices that order the lives of monks and nuns as they live in service to God. Depending on the specific monastic order (Franciscan, for instance, or Benedictine), this rule may commit its followers to values like poverty, chastity, stability, obedience, or conversion of life; it may call for saying the Daily Office seven times a day; it might outline the balance of work, prayer, and study that the community is to follow throughout each day.

Perhaps the best-known example is the Rule of St. Benedict of Nursia, a sixth-century monk and abbot who drew on even earlier sources to create what has become the model for many rules throughout the world. Benedict's Rule is a paragon of both rigor and moderation, sweeping principle and tiny detail: it describes not only a twelve-step path to humility but also the psalms to be said at specific times and the rotation for kitchen duty.

Rules of Life, however, are not just for nuns and monks. Many monasteries invite people outside their walls to become associates who adapt the monastic rule to their daily lives.[2] For example, the monks in my monastic order pray the Daily Office five times each day; I cannot fit that into my schedule, but I *can* pray the Office once a day, so that goes into my rule. Monks often hold all possessions in common; I can't do that, but I *can* commit to living simply and frugally, so that goes into my rule. By becoming an associate, you join a community of people (both nuns or monks and others) who have also dedicated themselves to living the rule; this can provide a vibrant source of support and accountability to help you grow in your practice.

Even so, you don't need to affiliate with a monastery to create and follow a Rule of Life. Some churches and other groups encourage their members to develop Rules of Life, and a wide range of resources can be found on the web. One of my favorite books on the spirit and practice of the rule is Joan Chittister's *Wisdom Distilled from the Daily: Living the Rule of St. Benedict Today,* which devotes one chapter to each of the primary values and practices of Benedict's Rule.[3]

But why do this at all? Over the years, I have come to think of my rule in terms of two metaphors: as an *anchor* and as a *framework.* In those periods when my life has turned upside down—through an insane work schedule, bouts of depression, relational turmoil, even those times when God simply seems absent—the daily call to practice my rule keeps me tethered to reality. It's not unlike living with animals: no matter how terrible you feel, the dogs need to be fed. Conversely, the rule anchors me during times of exhilaration, when I'm tempted to get too far ahead of myself. It is a reminder and an expression that God continues to work in the deepest recesses of our soul, day by day by day, whether we sense it or not.

Meanwhile, as a framework, the rule sets up a sort of scaffolding in which the movement of God takes place. Perhaps more correctly, it is where our *awareness* of that movement takes place. Daily prayer, reflection, and spiritual practice naturally fine-tune our antennae to the presence of God. The more sensitive we are to that presence, the more fully we can respond, and the deeper we go into the life of the spirit.

Other Practices

There are, of course, many other practices to help us draw closer to God and live according to God's will. To mention just two more:

Spiritual direction. Spiritual directors draw on their wisdom and experience with God, not to tell you what to do, but to help you hear God's voice. In essence, they listen *with* you to the movement of God in your life. Because we hear God so imperfectly—and never outside the bounds of our own perspective—connecting with a spiritual director can add an entirely different dimension to your reflections on the direction you are taking. One way to find a spiritual director in your area is to visit Spiritual Directors International (www.sdi.org).

Labyrinths. People have walked labyrinths for thousands of years, but interest in them seems to have surged in recent times. The labyrinth consists of a circle that encompasses a path toward the center, with many turns in the path along the way. You walk in and out—slowly, meditatively—along the same path.

Beyond these few basics, there is no "one right way" to walk a labyrinth. Some people focus on a prayer word, the Jesus prayer, or something similar. One version of the Jesus Prayer is "Lord Jesus Christ, Son of God, have mercy on me, a sinner," with each of the four phrases said in rhythm with the breath. Others might walk in intercession for a loved one or to reflect on a concern in their lives. I like to walk labyrinths with an empty mind, attentive to my surroundings and the movement of the Spirit within, lingering on anything that happens to arise. Often, during those times, I find my walk an exquisite, living metaphor for the spiritual life, with its continual turns (toward *and* away from my destination), the obstacles that thwart our progress, and a constant view of the ever-present center toward which we all travel.

You can start your labyrinth practice by locating a labyrinth near you. Visit the World-Wide Labyrinth Locator (www.labyrinthlocator.com) for help.

Notes

CHAPTER 1
When You Have to Move the Elephant

1. Robert Apatow, *The Spiritual Art of Dialogue: Mastering Communication for Personal Growth, Relationships, and the Workplace* (Rochester, Vt.: Inner Traditions, 1998), 3.
2. Improvisational artist Kat Koppett, in her book *Training to Imagine* (Sterling, Va.: Stylus Publishing, 2001), attributes this exercise to fellow artists Keith Johnstone, Viola Spolin, and the communities of Theatresports.
3. Apatow, *The Spiritual Art of Dialogue*, 3.
4. Leonard Swidler, *Theoria-Praxis: How Jews, Christians, and Muslims Can Together Move from Theory to Practice* (Leuven, Belgium: Uitgeverij Peeters, 1998), 24. Quoted in David R. Smock, ed., *Interfaith Dialogue and Peacebuilding* (Washington, D.C.: United States Institute of Peace Press, 2002), 6.
5. David Bohm, *On Dialogue* (New York and London: Routledge, 1996), 24.
6. Apatow, *The Spiritual Art of Dialogue,* 30.
7. William Isaacs, *Dialogue and the Art of Thinking Together* (New York: Currency, 1999).
8. Katz and Miller write extensively about the power of inclusion to help organizations achieve higher performance in *The Inclusion Breakthrough: Unleashing the Real Power of Diversity* (San Francisco: Berrett-Koehler Publishers, 2002). See, for example, "Inclusion: The HOW for the Next Organizational Breakthrough," *Practising Social Change* 5 (May 2012): 16–22. In the spirit of full disclosure, I am a proud employee of the consulting firm—The Kaleel Jamison Consulting Group, Inc.—where they serve as executive vice president and CEO, respectively.
9. "Church Leaders Discuss Human Sexuality," Public Conversations Project, www.publicconversations.org/dialogue/religious/anglican (accessed September 15, 2012).
10. Garret Keizer, "Turning Away from Jesus: Gay Rights and the War for the Episcopal Church," *Harper's Magazine*, June 2008, 48.
11. Really. Åsk Wäppling, "Casino Websites Paint Cows as Moo-ving Billboards," commercial-archive.com, August 10, 2005, http://commercial-archive.com/node/122451 (accessed June 26, 2012).

CHAPTER 2
Hearing the Call to Dialogue

1. Meister Eckhart, "We Are Children of God and Mothers of God," Sermon 23 in *Breakthrough: Meister Eckhart's Creation Spirituality in New Translation* (Garden City, N.Y.: Image Books, 1980), 325.

2. While quoting from the centurion story from Luke because of the details it provides, I take the chronology from the Gospel of Matthew. The story of the centurion appears in 8:5–13, and the story of the Canaanite woman appears in 15:21–28.

3. Wayne A. Meeks, gen. ed., *The HarperCollins Study Bible* (New York: HarperCollins Publishers, 1993), note to Mark 7:24.

4. Cullen Murphy, "Who Do Men Say That I Am?" *The Atlantic,* December 1986, www.theatlantic.com/magazine/archive/1986/12/ who-do-men-say-that-i-am/5710/ (accessed May 5, 2012).

5. The hymn with this title, written by the incomparable Charles Wesley in 1742, is a marvel of deep and childlike truth. I am taking issue not with the hymn, but with the notion that "gentle Jesus, meek and mild" could ever be his entire profile.

6. I have heard conservative commentators interpret this pejoratively, exemplifying a sinful lack of adherence to time-honored beliefs. However, I find it hard to condemn people who are "telling or hearing something new." Perhaps the fault, if any (and this may be the point of the author of Acts), lies in the notion of doing nothing *except* entertaining new ideas—a stance that indeed would be difficult for most Christians, with such a thorough grounding in an ancient scripture and millennia of tradition, to accept wholesale.

CHAPTER 3
Roadblocks on the Way

1. "Being wholly and verbally God-given, scripture is without error or fault in all its teaching, no less in what it states about God's acts in creation, about the events of world history, and about its own literary origins under God, than in its witness to God's saving grace in individual lives." "The Chicago Statement on Biblical Inerrancy," 1978, Center for Reformed Theology and Apologetics website, www.reformed.org/documents/index. html?mainframe=http://www.reformed.org/documents/icbi.html (accessed June 19, 2012).

2. For instance, "You shall not lie with a male as with a woman; it is an abomination" (Leviticus 18:22) and "Neither the immoral, nor idolaters, nor adulterers, nor homosexuals ... will inherit the kingdom of God" (1 Corinthians 6:9–10, Revised Standard Version). The New Revised

Standard Version replaces the word *homosexuals* with translations of the two original Greek words: *male prostitutes* and *sodomites*.

3. "Always to Care, Never to Kill," *The Wall Street Journal*, November 27, 1991, as presented at www.priestsforlife.org/euthanasia/alwaystocare.html (accessed June 26, 2012).

4. Ninette Sosa, Bob Franken, Rich Phillips, and Susan Candiotti, "Terri Schiavo Has Died," CNN.com, March 31, 2005, www.cnn.com/2005/LAW/03/31/schiavo/index.html (accessed June 26, 2012).

5. "Key News Audiences Now Blend Online and Traditional Sources," The Pew Research Center for the People & the Press, August 17, 2008, www.people-press.org/2008/08/17/key-news-audiences-now-blend-online-and-traditional-sources (accessed June 26, 2012).

6. Consider this observation from 2008: "But even [with] news about Iraq way down, coverage of that conflict still overshadows the Afghan struggle. From the beginning of this year through June 22, Iraq coverage registered at 4.7% of the newshole, generating six times more attention than news from the battlefields of Afghanistan." "The U.S. Media and the Other War," Pew Research Center's Project for Excellence in Journalism, June 25, 2008, www.journalism.org/node/11676 (accessed June 26, 2012).

7. John Consoli, "Nielsen: TV Viewing Grows," *Mediaweek*, September 21, 2006, www.mediaweek.com/mw/news/recent_display.jsp?vnu_content_id=1003154980.

8. For details on Clearness Committees, see Parker J. Palmer, "The Clearness Committee: A Communal Approach to Discernment," Center for Courage & Renewal, www.couragerenewal.org/parker/writings/clearness-committee (accessed June 26, 2012).

9. Christopher DeMuth, "Reaganomics: How's It Going?" American Enterprise Institute, August 28, 2006, www.aei.org/article/society-and-culture/reaganomics-hows-it-going (accessed June 26, 2012).

CHAPTER 4
Engaging the Work of the Soul

1. The term *LGBTQ* is a common abbreviation for *lesbian, gay, bisexual, transgendered, queer.*

2. "Franklin Graham: The Hell-Raising Evangelist's Son," *CBS Sunday Morning*, April 8, 2012, www.cbsnews.com/8301-3445_162-57410991/franklin-graham-the-hell-raising-evangelists-son (accessed August 25, 2012).

3. Please see Suggestions for Further Reading section for some of my recommendations.

4. For a good overview of Christian centering prayer, see the authoritative source on the subject, Contemplative Outreach, Ltd., especially the

"Centering Prayer" web page at www.centeringprayer.com/cntrgpryr.htm (accessed June 26, 2012).

5. Jackie Smallbones, "Quiet Time Lessons," *Church Herald*, March 1999.

6. Many writers have described the process of *lectio divina*. For a very good introduction to the practice, see "What Is Lectio Divina?" at the official website of the Carmelite Order, http://ocarm.org/en/content/lectio/what-lectio-divina (accessed June 26, 2012).

CHAPTER 5
Three Mind-Sets for the Journey

1. Gil Fronsdal, "Not-Knowing," Insight Meditation Center website, www.insightmeditationcenter.org/books-articles/articles/not-knowing (accessed May 17, 2012).

2. Brian Montopoli, "Tea Party Supporters: Who They Are and What They Believe," CBS News, April 14, 2010, www.cbsnews.com/8301-503544_162-20002529-503544.html (accessed May 26, 2012).

3. Nanette Gartrell, MD, and Henny Bos, PhD, "U.S. National Longitudinal Lesbian Family Study: Psychological Adjustment of 17-Year-Old Adolescents," *Pediatrics*, June 7, 2010, http://pediatrics.aappublications.org/content/early/2010/06/07/peds.2009-3153.abstract#aff-1 (accessed May 26, 2012).

4. The BothAnd Project has ceased operations, but Joshua Weiss, a cofounder and senior fellow of the Global Negotiation Initiative, told me that the quote "very much still infuses much of our work in other realms" (Joshua N. Weiss e-mail to John Backman, May 24, 2012).

CHAPTER 6
Pushing beyond Our Borders

1. See, for instance, Energy Information Administration, U.S. Department of Energy, "Analysis of Crude Oil Production in the Arctic National Wildlife Refuge," www.eia.gov/oiaf/servicerpt/anwr/pdf/sroiaf%282008%2903.pdf (accessed June 26, 2012).

2. "The 2% Illusion," *The Wall Street Journal,* February 27, 2009, http://online.wsj.com/article/SB123561551065378405.html?mod=djemEditorialPage (accessed June 26, 2012).

3. For an overview of this topic, see Jeanne Segal with Jaelline Jaffe, "Relationships and Brain Evolution," Helpguide.org, October 2008, www.helpguide.org/mental/eqb_social_emotional_brain.htm (accessed June 26, 2012). The work of Daniel J. Siegel, a key figure in the field of interpersonal neurobiology, is particularly important here. A brief

introduction to his research may be found at "Toward an Interpersonal Neurobiology of the Developing Mind," *Infant Mental Health Journal* 22 (2001): 67-94, http://onlinelibrary.wiley.com/doi/10.1002/1097-0355%28200101/04%2922:1%3C67::AID-IMHJ3%3E3.0.CO;2-G/abstract (accessed June 26, 2012).

4. John Backman, "C-GCC Educator Encounters the New Hungary," *Columbia-Greene Community College Credit & Noncredit Classes*, Spring 2000, 3.

5. The idea that the Inuit have one hundred words for snow would illustrate the point as well: when you live with something so intimately, you begin to see extremely subtle differences in it and express them in language. Unfortunately, the "one hundred words for snow" is a myth. The reality is far more complex: see, for example, Geoffrey K. Pullum, "Sasha Aikhenvald on Inuit Snow Words: A Clarification," Language Log, January 30, 2004, http://itre.cis.upenn.edu/~myl/languagelog/archives/000405.html (accessed June 26, 2012).

6. No, it doesn't exist—at least not that I can determine. Thanks be to God.

7. "Why Russia Still Loves Stalin," *The Washington Post,* February 12, 2006, www.washingtonpost.com/wp-dyn/content/article/2006/02/11/AR2006021100845.html (accessed June 26, 2012).

8. Mark Twain, *Following the Equator*, rev. ed. (Whitefish, Mont.: Kessinger Publishing, 2004), 66.

CHAPTER 7
Making Dialogue Happen

1. See, for instance, Tanya Bartrand and John Bargh, "The Chameleon Effect: The Perception-Behavior Link and Social Interaction," *Journal of Personality and Social Psychology* 76 (1999): 893–910, http://psycnet.apa.org/index.cfm?fa=buy.optionToBuy&id=1999-05479-002 (accessed June 26, 2012).

2. Roger Ailes with Jon Kraushar, *You Are the Message* (New York: Doubleday, 1988), 47–48.

3. Parker J. Palmer, "The Clearness Committee: A Communal Approach to Discernment," Center for Courage & Renewal, www.couragerenewal.org/parker/writings/clearness-committee (accessed June 26, 2012).

4. Howard Luck Gossage, "Is There Any Hope for Advertising?" in *The Book of Gossage: A Compilation* (Chicago: The Copy Workshop, 1995), 38.

CHAPTER 8
Dialogue Unbound

1. *Sharm El-Sheikh Fact-Finding Committee Report,* special report prepared at the request of the U.S. Department of State, April 30, 2001, www.state.gov/p/nea/rls/rpt/3060.htm.
2. "Statistics: Fatalities," B'Tselem (The Israeli Information Center for Human Rights in the Occupied Territories), http://old.btselem.org/statistics/english/Casualties.asp (accessed June 26, 2012).
3. Marcus Borg, *Reading the Bible Again for the First Time* (New York: HarperCollins, 2001), 22.
4. *The Cocktail Party* (Orlando: Harcourt Brace & Company, 1950), 71–72.

CHAPTER 9
Dialogue in the War Zone

1. This section draws on several accounts of the events described here. See, for instance, Anne Fowler, Nicki Nichols Gamble, Frances X. Hogan, Melissa Kogut, Madeline McComish, and Barbara Thorp, "Talking with the Enemy," *Boston Sunday Globe,* January 28, 2001, F1, http://pubpages.unh.edu/~jds/BostonGlobe.htm (accessed June 26, 2012); "Getting Started: PCP's First Dialogues," Public Conversations Project, www.publicconversations.org/who/firstdialogues; "Dialogue on Abortion Among Pro-Life and Pro-Choice Leaders in Conjunction with the Public Conversations Project," Susan Podziba & Associates website, http://podziba.com/abortiondialoguecase.html; "Beyond the Abortion Debate: Common Ground," The Co-Intelligence Institute website, www.co-intelligence.org/S-beyondabortiondebate.html; Mary Jacksteit, "The Buffalo Case: Pro-Life and Pro-Choice Can Work Together," *The Huffington Post,* June 15, 2009, www.huffingtonpost.com/mary-jacksteit/the-buffalo-case-pro-life_b_215067.html. All sites accessed June 12, 2012 except where noted.
2. The state of the abortion controversy is such that even the language used by one side to describe *itself* is offensive to the other side. Throughout this section, I use language like *pro-choice* and *pro-life* not because I believe they are accurate, but purely for the sake of communicating in widely used terms without distracting from the main story.

EPILOGUE
A Gentle Challenge to Our Culture

1. John J. Macionis, *Sociology,* 14th ed. (New York: Pearson, 2012), 66, searched at www.coursesmart.com/9780205116683/CH-1# (accessed June 25, 2012).

APPENDIX
Spiritual Practices for the Way of Dialogue

1. Mark Buetow, "Using the *Brotherhood Prayer Book*," Lutheran Liturgical Prayer Brotherhood, Lent 2005, www.llpb.us/PDFs/UsingBPB-Mark%20Beutow.pdf (accessed July 16, 2012).

2. Holy Cross Monastery, where I am an associate, publishes its own Associates' Rule, which associates adapt even further to fit the unique circumstances of their lives. You can find it at www.holycrossmonastery.com/associates/the-associates-rule (accessed July 21, 2012).

3. New York: HarperCollins, 1990. A Benedictine sister, prolific author, and internationally known lecturer, Chittister writes about spiritual topics with a depth of insight that makes any of her books worth the read. More information on her can be found at www.benetvision.org/vitaJoan.html (accessed July 21, 2012).

Suggestions for Further Reading

Books on Spiritual Practice

Bianco, Frank. *Voices of Silence: Lives of the Trappists Today*. New York: Anchor Books, 1991.

Chittister, Joan. *Wisdom Distilled from the Daily: Living the Rule of St. Benedict Today*. San Francisco: Harper & Row, 1990.

Merton, Thomas. *Contemplative Prayer*. New York: Doubleday Religion, 1969.

———. *No Man Is an Island*. Boston: Shambhala Publications, 1955.

Paintner, Christine Valters. *Lectio Divina—The Sacred Art: Transforming Words and Images into Heart-Centered Prayer*. Woodstock, VT: SkyLight Paths Publishing, 2011.

Palmer, Parker J. *A Hidden Wholeness: The Journey toward an Undivided Life*. San Francisco: Jossey-Bass, 2004.

Pennington, M. Basil, Thomas Keating, and Thomas E. Clarke. *Finding Grace at the Center: The Beginning of Centering Prayer*. 3d ed. Woodstock, VT: SkyLight Paths Publishing, 2007.

Books Related to Dialogue

Apatow, Robert. *The Spiritual Art of Dialogue: Mastering Communication for Personal Growth, Relationships, and the Workplace*. Rochester, VT: Inner Traditions, 1998.

Bohm, David. *On Dialogue*. New York: Routledge, 1996.

Brown, Juanita, with William Isaacs and The World Café Community. *The World Café: Shaping Our Futures through Conversations That Matter*. San Francisco: Berrett-Koehler Publishers, 2005.

Hacala, Sara. *Saving Civility: 52 Ways to Tame Rude, Crude and Attitude for a Polite Planet*. Woodstock, VT: SkyLight Paths Publishing, 2011.

Isaacs, William. *Dialogue and the Art of Thinking Together*. New York: Doubleday, 1999.

Palmer, Parker J. *Healing the Heart of Democracy: The Courage to Create a Politics Worthy of the Human Spirit*. San Francisco: Jossey-Bass, 2011.

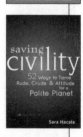
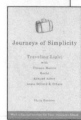

Bible Stories / Folktales

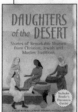

Abraham's Bind & Other Bible Tales of Trickery, Folly, Mercy and Love by Michael J. Caduto

New retellings of episodes in the lives of familiar biblical characters explore relevant life lessons. 6 x 9, 224 pp, HC, 978-1-59473-186-0 **$19.99**

Daughters of the Desert: Stories of Remarkable Women from Christian, Jewish and Muslim Traditions by Claire Rudolf Murphy,

Meghan Nuttall Sayres, Mary Cronk Farrell, Sarah Conover and Betsy Wharton

Breathes new life into the old tales of our female ancestors in faith. Uses traditional scriptural passages as starting points, then with vivid detail fills in historical context and place. Chapters reveal the voices of Sarah, Hagar, Huldah, Esther, Salome, Mary Magdalene, Lydia, Khadija, Fatima and many more. Historical fiction ideal for readers of all ages.

5½ x 8½, 192 pp, Quality PB, 978-1-59473-106-8 **$14.99** Inc. reader's discussion guide
HC, 978-1-893361-72-0 **$19.95**

The Triumph of Eve & Other Subversive Bible Tales
by Matt Biers-Ariel

These engaging retellings of familiar Bible stories are witty, often hilarious and always profound. They invite you to grapple with questions and issues that are often hidden in the original texts.

5½ x 8½, 192 pp, Quality PB, 978-1-59473-176-1 **$14.99**

Also available: **The Triumph of Eve Teacher's Guide**
8½ x 11, 44 pp, PB, 978-1-59473-152-5 **$8.99**

Wisdom in the Telling

Finding Inspiration and Grace in Traditional Folktales and Myths Retold
by Lorraine Hartin-Gelardi
6 x 9, 192 pp, HC, 978-1-59473-185-3 **$19.99**

Religious Etiquette / Reference

How to Be a Perfect Stranger, 5th Edition: The Essential Religious Etiquette Handbook Edited by Stuart M. Matlins and Arthur J. Magida

The indispensable guidebook to help the well-meaning guest when visiting other people's religious ceremonies. A straightforward guide to the rituals and celebrations of the major religions and denominations in the United States and Canada from the perspective of an interested guest of any other faith, based on information obtained from authorities of each religion. Belongs in every living room, library and office. Covers:

African American Methodist Churches • Assemblies of God • Bahá'í Faith • Baptist • Buddhist • Christian Church (Disciples of Christ) • Christian Science (Church of Christ, Scientist) • Churches of Christ • Episcopalian and Anglican • Hindu • Islam • Jehovah's Witnesses • Jewish • Lutheran • Mennonite/Amish • Methodist • Mormon (Church of Jesus Christ of Latter-day Saints) • Native American/First Nations • Orthodox Churches • Pentecostal Church of God • Presbyterian • Quaker (Religious Society of Friends) • Reformed Church in America/Canada • Roman Catholic • Seventh-day Adventist • Sikh • Unitarian Universalist • United Church of Canada • United Church of Christ

"The things Miss Manners forgot to tell us about religion."

—*Los Angeles Times*

"Finally, for those inclined to undertake their own spiritual journeys ... tells visitors what to expect."　　　　　—*New York Times*

6 x 9, 432 pp, Quality PB, 978-1-59473-294-2 **$19.99**

The Perfect Stranger's Guide to Funerals and Grieving Practices: A Guide to Etiquette in Other People's Religious Ceremonies Edited by Stuart M. Matlins
6 x 9, 240 pp, Quality PB, 978-1-893361-20-1 **$16.95**

The Perfect Stranger's Guide to Wedding Ceremonies: A Guide to Etiquette in Other People's Religious Ceremonies Edited by Stuart M. Matlins
6 x 9, 208 pp, Quality PB, 978-1-893361-19-5 **$16.95**

Sacred Texts—SkyLight Illuminations Series

Offers today's spiritual seeker an enjoyable entry into the great classic texts of the world's spiritual traditions. Each classic is presented in an accessible translation, with facing pages of guided commentary from experts, giving you the keys you need to understand the history, context and meaning of the text.

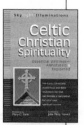

CHRISTIANITY

Celtic Christian Spirituality: Essential Writings—Annotated & Explained
Annotation by Mary C. Earle; Foreword by John Philip Newell
Explores how the writings of this lively tradition embody the gospel.
5½ x 8½, 176 pp, Quality PB, 978-1-59473-302-4 **$16.99**

Desert Fathers and Mothers: Early Christian Wisdom Sayings—
Annotated & Explained
Annotation by Christine Valters Paintner, PhD
Opens up wisdom of the desert fathers and mothers for readers with no previous knowledge of Western monasticism and early Christianity.
5½ x 8½, 192 pp, Quality PB, 978-1-59473-373-4 **$16.99**

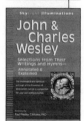

The End of Days: Essential Selections from Apocalyptic Texts—
Annotated & Explained
Annotation by Robert G. Clouse, PhD
Helps you understand the complex Christian visions of the end of the world.
5½ x 8½, 224 pp, Quality PB, 978-1-59473-170-9 **$16.99**

The Hidden Gospel of Matthew: Annotated & Explained
Translation & Annotation by Ron Miller
Discover the words and events that have the strongest connection to the historical Jesus.
5½ x 8½, 272 pp, Quality PB, 978-1-59473-038-2 **$16.99**

The Infancy Gospels of Jesus: Apocryphal Tales from the Childhoods of Mary and Jesus—Annotated & Explained
Translation & Annotation by Stevan Davies; Foreword by A. Edward Siecienski, PhD
A startling presentation of the early lives of Mary, Jesus and other biblical figures that will amuse and surprise you.
5½ x 8½, 176 pp, Quality PB, 978-1-59473-258-4 **$16.99**

John & Charles Wesley: Selections from Their Writings and Hymns—
Annotated & Explained
Annotation by Paul W. Chilcote, PhD
A unique presentation of the writings of these two inspiring brothers brings together some of the most essential material from their large corpus of work.
5½ x 8½, 288 pp, Quality PB, 978-1-59473-309-3 **$16.99**

The Lost Sayings of Jesus: Teachings from Ancient Christian, Jewish, Gnostic and Islamic Sources—Annotated & Explained
Translation & Annotation by Andrew Phillip Smith; Foreword by Stephan A. Hoeller
This collection of more than three hundred sayings depicts Jesus as a Wisdom teacher who speaks to people of all faiths as a mystic and spiritual master.
5½ x 8½, 240 pp, Quality PB, 978-1-59473-172-3 **$16.99**

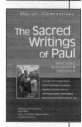

Philokalia: The Eastern Christian Spiritual Texts—Selections
Annotated & Explained *Annotation by Allyne Smith; Translation by G. E. H. Palmer, Phillip Sherrard and Bishop Kallistos Ware*
The first approachable introduction to the wisdom of the Philokalia, the classic text of Eastern Christian spirituality.
5½ x 8½, 240 pp, Quality PB, 978-1-59473-103-7 **$16.99**

The Sacred Writings of Paul: Selections Annotated & Explained
Translation & Annotation by Ron Miller
Leads you into the exciting immediacy of Paul's teachings.
5½ x 8½, 224 pp, Quality PB, 978-1-59473-213-3 **$16.99**

Sacred Texts—continued

CHRISTIANITY—continued

Saint Augustine of Hippo: Selections from *Confessions* and Other Essential Writings—Annotated & Explained
Annotation by Joseph T. Kelley, PhD; Translation by the Augustinian Heritage Institute
Provides insight into the mind and heart of this foundational Christian figure.
5½ x 8½, 272 pp, Quality PB, 978-1-59473-282-9 **$16.99**

Saint Ignatius Loyola—The Spiritual Writings: Selections Annotated & Explained *Annotation by Mark Mossa, SJ*
Draws from contemporary translations of original texts focusing on the practical mysticism of Ignatius of Loyola.
5½ x 8½, 288 pp, Quality PB, 978-1-59473-301-7 **$16.99**

Sex Texts from the Bible: Selections Annotated & Explained
Translation & Annotation by Teresa J. Hornsby; Foreword by Amy-Jill Levine
Demystifies the Bible's ideas on gender roles, marriage, sexual orientation, virginity, lust and sexual pleasure.
5½ x 8½, 208 pp, Quality PB, 978-1-59473-217-1 **$16.99**

Spiritual Writings on Mary: Annotated & Explained
Annotation by Mary Ford-Grabowsky; Foreword by Andrew Harvey
Examines the role of Mary, the mother of Jesus, as a source of inspiration in history and in life today.
5½ x 8½, 288 pp, Quality PB, 978-1-59473-001-6 **$16.99**

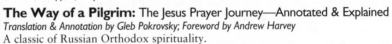

The Way of a Pilgrim: The Jesus Prayer Journey—Annotated & Explained
Translation & Annotation by Gleb Pokrovsky; Foreword by Andrew Harvey
A classic of Russian Orthodox spirituality.
5½ x 8½, 160 pp, Illus., Quality PB, 978-1-893361-31-7 **$14.95**

GNOSTICISM

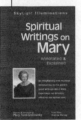

Gnostic Writings on the Soul: Annotated & Explained
Translation & Annotation by Andrew Phillip Smith; Foreword by Stephan A. Hoeller
Reveals the inspiring ways your soul can remember and return to its unique, divine purpose.
5½ x 8½, 144 pp, Quality PB, 978-1-59473-220-1 **$16.99**

The Gospel of Philip: Annotated & Explained
Translation & Annotation by Andrew Phillip Smith; Foreword by Stevan Davies
Reveals otherwise unrecorded sayings of Jesus and fragments of Gnostic mythology.
5½ x 8½, 160 pp, Quality PB, 978-1-59473-111-2 **$16.99**

The Gospel of Thomas: Annotated & Explained
Translation & Annotation by Stevan Davies; Foreword by Andrew Harvey
Sheds new light on the origins of Christianity and portrays Jesus as a wisdom-loving sage.
5½ x 8½, 192 pp, Quality PB, 978-1-893361-45-4 **$16.99**

The Secret Book of John: The Gnostic Gospel—Annotated & Explained
Translation & Annotation by Stevan Davies
The most significant and influential text of the ancient Gnostic religion.
5½ x 8½, 208 pp, Quality PB, 978-1-59473-082-5 **$16.99**

Children's Spirituality

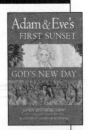

Adam & Eve's First Sunset: God's New Day
by Sandy Eisenberg Sasso; Full-color illus. by Joani Keller Rothenberg 9 x 12, 32 pp, Full-color illus.,
HC, 978-1-58023-177-0 **$17.95*** *For ages 4 & up*

Because Nothing Looks Like God
by Lawrence Kushner and Karen Kushner; Full-color illus. by Dawn W. Majewski
Invites parents and children to explore the questions we all have about God.
11 x 8½, 32 pp, Full-color illus., HC, 978-1-58023-092-6 **$17.99*** *For ages 4 & up*

Also available: **Teacher's Guide** 8½ x 11, 22 pp, PB, 978-1-58023-140-4 **$6.95**

But God Remembered: Stories of Women from Creation to the
Promised Land *by Sandy Eisenberg Sasso; Full-color illus. by Bethanne Andersen*
A fascinating collection of four different stories of women only briefly mentioned in biblical tradition and religious texts.
9 x 12, 32 pp, Full-color illus., Quality PB, 978-1-58023-372-9 **$8.99*** *For ages 8 & up*

Cain & Abel: Finding the Fruits of Peace
by Sandy Eisenberg Sasso; Full-color illus. by Joani Keller Rothenberg
A sensitive recasting of the ancient tale shows we have the power to deal with anger
in positive ways. "Editor's Choice." —American Library Association's *Booklist*
9 x 12, 32 pp, Full-color illus., HC, 978-1-58023-123-7 **$16.95*** *For ages 5 & up*

Does God Hear My Prayer?
by August Gold; Full-color photos by Diane Hardy Waller
Introduces preschoolers and young readers to prayer and how it helps them
express their own emotions.
10 x 8½, 32 pp, Full-color photo illus., Quality PB, 978-1-59473-102-0 **$8.99** *For ages 3–6*

The 11th Commandment: Wisdom from Our Children *by The Children of America*
"If there were an Eleventh Commandment, what would it be?" Children of many
religious denominations across America answer this question—in their own draw-
ings and words. "A rare book of spiritual celebration for all people, of all ages,
for all time." —*Bookviews* 8 x 10, 48 pp, Full-color illus., HC, 978-1-879045-46-0 **$16.95***
For all ages

For Heaven's Sake *by Sandy Eisenberg Sasso; Full-color illus. by Kathryn Kunz Finney*
Heaven is often found where you least expect it.
9 x 12, 32 pp, Full-color illus., HC, 978-1-58023-054-4 **$16.95*** *For ages 4 & up*

God in Between *by Sandy Eisenberg Sasso; Full-color illus. by Sally Sweetland*
A magical, mythical tale that teaches that God can be found where we are.
9 x 12, 32 pp, Full-color illus., HC, 978-1-879045-86-6 **$16.95*** *For ages 4 & up*

God's Paintbrush: Special 10th Anniversary Edition
by Sandy Eisenberg Sasso; Full-color illus. by Annette Compton
Invites children of all faiths and backgrounds to encounter God through moments
in their own lives. 11 x 8½, 32 pp, Full-color illus., HC, 978-1-58023-195-4 **$17.95*** *For ages 4 & up*

Also available: **God's Paintbrush Teacher's Guide**
8½ x 11, 32 pp, PB, 978-1-879045-57-6 **$8.95**

God's Paintbrush Celebration Kit: A Spiritual Activity Kit for Teachers and
Students of All Faiths, All Backgrounds 9½ x 12, 40 Full-color Activity Sheets & Teacher
Folder w/ complete instructions, HC, 978-1-58023-050-6 **$21.95**
Additional activity sheets available:
8-Student Activity Sheet Pack (40 sheets/5 sessions), 978-1-58023-058-2 **$19.95**
Single-Student Activity Sheet Pack (5 sessions), 978-1-58023-059-9 **$3.95**

I Am God's Paintbrush (A Board Book)
by Sandy Eisenberg Sasso; Full-color illus. by Annette Compton
5 x 5, 24 pp, Full-color illus., Board Book, 978-1-59473-265-2 **$7.99** *For ages 0–4*

* A book from Jewish Lights, SkyLight Paths' sister imprint

Children's Spirituality

Remembering My Grandparent: A Kid's Own Grief Workbook in the Christian Tradition *by Nechama Liss-Levinson, PhD, and Rev. Molly Phinney Baskette, MDiv* 8 x 10, 48 pp, 2-color text, HC, 978-1-59473-212-6 **$16.99** *For ages 7 & up*

Does God Ever Sleep? *by Joan Sauro, CSJ*
A charming nighttime reminder that God is always present in our lives.
10 x 8½, 32 pp, Full-color photos, Quality PB, 978-1-59473-110-5 **$8.99** *For ages 3–6*

Does God Forgive Me? *by August Gold; Full-color photos by Diane Hardy Waller*
Gently shows how God forgives all that we do if we are truly sorry.
10 x 8½, 32 pp, Full-color photos, Quality PB, 978-1-59473-142-6 **$8.99** *For ages 3–6*

God Said Amen *by Sandy Eisenberg Sasso; Full-color illus. by Avi Katz*
A warm and inspiring tale that shows us that we need only reach out to each other to find the answers to our prayers.
9 x 12, 32 pp, Full-color illus., HC, 978-1-58023-080-3 **$16.95*** *For ages 4 & up*

How Does God Listen? *by Kay Lindahl; Full-color photos by Cynthia Maloney*
How do we know when God is listening to us? Children will find the answers to these questions as they engage their senses while the story unfolds, learning how God listens in the wind, waves, clouds, hot chocolate, perfume, our tears and our laughter.
10 x 8½, 32 pp, Full-color photos, Quality PB, 978-1-59473-084-9 **$8.99** *For ages 3–6*

In God's Hands *by Lawrence Kushner and Gary Schmidt; Full-color illus. by Matthew J. Baek*
9 x 12, 32 pp, Full-color illus., HC, 978-1-58023-224-1 **$16.99*** *For ages 5 & up*

In God's Name *by Sandy Eisenberg Sasso; Full-color illus. by Phoebe Stone*
Like an ancient myth in its poetic text and vibrant illustrations, this award-winning modern fable about the search for God's name celebrates the diversity and, at the same time, the unity of all the people of the world.
9 x 12, 32 pp, Full-color illus., HC, 978-1-879045-26-2 **$16.99*** *For ages 4 & up*

Also available in Spanish: El nombre de Dios
9 x 12, 32 pp, Full-color illus., HC, 978-1-893361-63-8 **$16.95**

In Our Image: God's First Creatures
by Nancy Sohn Swartz; Full-color illus. by Melanie Hall
A playful new twist on the Genesis story—from the perspective of the animals. Celebrates the interconnectedness of nature and the harmony of all living things.
9 x 12, 32 pp, Full-color illus., HC, 978-1-879045-99-6 **$16.95*** *For ages 4 & up*

Noah's Wife: The Story of Naamah
by Sandy Eisenberg Sasso; Full-color illus. by Bethanne Andersen
Opens young readers' religious imaginations to new ideas about the well-known story of the Flood. When God tells Noah to bring the animals of the world onto the ark, God also calls on Naamah, Noah's wife, to save each plant on Earth.
9 x 12, 32 pp, Full-color illus., HC, 978-1-58023-134-3 **$16.95*** *For ages 4 & up*

Also available: Naamah: Noah's Wife (A Board Book)
by Sandy Eisenberg Sasso; Full-color illus. by Bethanne Andersen
5 x 5, 24 pp, Full-color illus., Board Book, 978-1-893361-56-0 **$7.95** *For ages 0–4*

Where Does God Live? *by August Gold and Matthew J. Perlman*
Helps children and their parents find God in the world around us with simple, practical examples children can relate to.
10 x 8½, 32 pp, Full-color photos, Quality PB, 978-1-893361-39-3 **$8.99** *For ages 3–6*

* A book from Jewish Lights, SkyLight Paths' sister imprint

Spirituality of the Seasons

Autumn: A Spiritual Biography of the Season
Edited by Gary Schmidt and Susan M. Felch; Illus. by Mary Azarian
Rejoice in autumn as a time of preparation and reflection. Includes Wendell Berry, David James Duncan, Robert Frost, A. Bartlett Giamatti, E. B. White, P. D. James, Julian of Norwich, Garret Keizer, Tracy Kidder, Anne Lamott, May Sarton.
6 x 9, 320 pp, b/w illus., Quality PB, 978-1-59473-118-1 **$18.99**

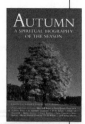

Spring: A Spiritual Biography of the Season
Edited by Gary Schmidt and Susan M. Felch; Illus. by Mary Azarian
Explore the gentle unfurling of spring and reflect on how nature celebrates rebirth and renewal. Includes Jane Kenyon, Lucy Larcom, Harry Thurston, Nathaniel Hawthorne, Noel Perrin, Annie Dillard, Martha Ballard, Barbara Kingsolver, Dorothy Wordsworth, Donald Hall, David Brill, Lionel Basney, Isak Dinesen, Paul Laurence Dunbar. 6 x 9, 352 pp, b/w illus., Quality PB, 978-1-59473-246-1 **$18.99**

Summer: A Spiritual Biography of the Season
Edited by Gary Schmidt and Susan M. Felch; Illus. by Barry Moser
"A sumptuous banquet.... These selections lift up an exquisite wholeness found within an everyday sophistication." — ★ *Publishers Weekly* starred review
Includes Anne Lamott, Luci Shaw, Ray Bradbury, Richard Selzer, Thomas Lynch, Walt Whitman, Carl Sandburg, Sherman Alexie, Madeleine L'Engle, Jamaica Kincaid.
6 x 9, 304 pp, b/w illus., Quality PB, 978-1-59473-183-9 **$18.99**
HC, 978-1-59473-083-2 **$21.99**

Winter: A Spiritual Biography of the Season
Edited by Gary Schmidt and Susan M. Felch; Illus. by Barry Moser
"This outstanding anthology features top-flight nature and spirituality writers on the fierce, inexorable season of winter.... Remarkably lively and warm, despite the icy subject." — ★ *Publishers Weekly* starred review
Includes Will Campbell, Rachel Carson, Annie Dillard, Donald Hall, Ron Hansen, Jane Kenyon, Jamaica Kincaid, Barry Lopez, Kathleen Norris, John Updike, E. B. White.
6 x 9, 288 pp, b/w illus., Deluxe PB w/ flaps, 978-1-893361-92-8 **$18.95**
HC, 978-1-893361-53-9 **$21.95**

Spirituality / Animal Companions

Blessing the Animals: Prayers and Ceremonies to Celebrate God's Creatures, Wild and Tame *Edited and with Introductions by Lynn L. Caruso*
5¼ x 7¼, 256 pp, Quality PB, 978-1-59473-253-9 **$15.99**; HC, 978-1-59473-145-7 **$19.99**

Remembering My Pet: A Kid's Own Spiritual Workbook for When a Pet Dies
by Nechama Liss-Levinson, PhD, and Rev. Molly Phinney Baskette, MDiv; Foreword by Lynn L. Caruso
8 x 10, 48 pp, 2-color text, HC, 978-1-59473-221-8 **$16.99**

What Animals Can Teach Us about Spirituality: Inspiring Lessons from Wild and Tame Creatures *by Diana L. Guerrero* 6 x 9, 176 pp, Quality PB, 978-1-893361-84-3 **$16.95**

Spirituality—A Week Inside

Lighting the Lamp of Wisdom: A Week Inside a Yoga Ashram
by John Ittner; Foreword by Dr. David Frawley
6 x 9, 192 pp, b/w photos, Quality PB, 978-1-893361-52-2 **$15.95**

Making a Heart for God: A Week Inside a Catholic Monastery
by Dianne Aprile; Foreword by Brother Patrick Hart, OCSO
6 x 9, 224 pp, b/w photos, Quality PB, 978-1-893361-49-2 **$16.95**

Waking Up: A Week Inside a Zen Monastery
by Jack Maguire; Foreword by John Daido Loori, Roshi
6 x 9, 224 pp, b/w photos, Quality PB, 978-1-893361-55-3 **$16.95**; HC, 978-1-893361-13-3 **$21.95**

Spiritual Poetry—The Mystic Poets

Experience these mystic poets as you never have before. Each beautiful, compact book includes a brief introduction to the poet's time and place, a summary of the major themes of the poet's mysticism and religious tradition, essential selections from the poet's most important works, and an appreciative preface by a contemporary spiritual writer.

Hafiz
The Mystic Poets
Translated and with Notes by Gertrude Bell
Preface by Ibrahim Gamard
Hafiz is known throughout the world as Persia's greatest poet, with sales of his poems in Iran today only surpassed by those of the Qur'an itself. His probing and joyful verse speaks to people from all backgrounds who long to taste and feel divine love and experience harmony with all living things.
5 x 7¼, 144 pp, HC, 978-1-59473-009-2 **$16.99**

Hopkins
The Mystic Poets
Preface by Rev. Thomas Ryan, CSP
Gerard Manley Hopkins, Christian mystical poet, is beloved for his use of fresh language and startling metaphors to describe the world around him. Although his verse is lovely, beneath the surface lies a searching soul, wrestling with and yearning for God.
5 x 7¼, 112 pp, HC, 978-1-59473-010-8 **$16.99**

Tagore
The Mystic Poets
Preface by Swami Adiswarananda
Rabindranath Tagore is often considered the Shakespeare of modern India. A great mystic, Tagore was the teacher of W. B. Yeats and Robert Frost, the close friend of Albert Einstein and Mahatma Gandhi, and the winner of the Nobel Prize for Literature. This beautiful sampling of Tagore's two most important works, *The Gardener* and *Gitanjali,* offers a glimpse into his spiritual vision that has inspired people around the world.
5 x 7¼, 144 pp, HC, 978-1-59473-008-5 **$16.99**

Whitman
The Mystic Poets
Preface by Gary David Comstock
Walt Whitman was the most innovative and influential poet of the nineteenth century. This beautiful sampling of Whitman's most important poetry from *Leaves of Grass,* and selections from his prose writings, offers a glimpse into the spiritual side of his most radical themes—love for country, love for others and love of self.
5 x 7¼, 192 pp, HC, 978-1-59473-041-2 **$16.99**

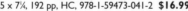

Spiritual Practice

Fly-Fishing—The Sacred Art: Casting a Fly as a Spiritual Practice
by Rabbi Eric Eisenkramer and Rev. Michael Attas, MD; Foreword by Chris Wood, CEO,
Trout Unlimited; Preface by Lori Simon, executive director, Casting for Recovery
Shares what fly-fishing can teach you about reflection, awe and wonder; the benefits
of solitude; the blessing of community and the search for the Divine.
5½ x 8½, 160 pp, Quality PB, 978-1-59473-299-7 **$16.99**

Lectio Divina—The Sacred Art: Transforming Words & Images into
Heart-Centered Prayer *by Christine Valters Paintner, PhD*
Expands the practice of sacred reading beyond scriptural texts and makes it
accessible in contemporary life. 5½ x 8½, 240 pp, Quality PB, 978-1-59473-300-0 **$16.99**

Writing—The Sacred Art: Beyond the Page to Spiritual Practice
By Rami Shapiro and Aaron Shapiro
Push your writing through the trite and the boring to something fresh, something
transformative. Includes over fifty unique, practical exercises.
5½ x 8½, 192 pp, Quality PB, 978-1-59473-372-7 **$16.99**

Dance—The Sacred Art: The Joy of Movement as a Spiritual Practice
by Cynthia Winton-Henry 5½ x 8½, 224 pp, Quality PB, 978-1-59473-268-3 **$16.99**

Everyday Herbs in Spiritual Life: A Guide to Many Practices
by Michael J. Caduto; Foreword by Rosemary Gladstar
7 x 9, 208 pp, 20+ b/w illus., Quality PB, 978-1-59473-174-7 **$16.99**

Giving—The Sacred Art: Creating a Lifestyle of Generosity
by Lauren Tyler Wright 5½ x 8½, 208 pp, Quality PB, 978-1-59473-224-9 **$16.99**

Haiku—The Sacred Art: A Spiritual Practice in Three Lines
by Margaret D. McGee 5½ x 8½, 192 pp, Quality PB, 978-1-59473-269-0 **$16.99**

Hospitality—The Sacred Art: Discovering the Hidden Spiritual Power of Invitation
and Welcome *by Rev. Nanette Sawyer; Foreword by Rev. Dirk Ficca*
5½ x 8½, 208 pp, Quality PB, 978-1-59473-228-7 **$16.99**

Labyrinths from the Outside In: Walking to Spiritual Insight—A Beginner's Guide
by Donna Schaper and Carole Ann Camp
6 x 9, 208 pp, b/w illus. and photos, Quality PB, 978-1-893361-18-8 **$16.95**

Practicing the Sacred Art of Listening: A Guide to Enrich Your Relationships
and Kindle Your Spiritual Life *by Kay Lindahl* 8 x 8, 176 pp, Quality PB, 978-1-893361-85-0 **$16.95**

Recovery—The Sacred Art: The Twelve Steps as Spiritual Practice *by Rami Shapiro;*
Foreword by Joan Borysenko, PhD 5½ x 8½, 240 pp, Quality PB, 978-1-59473-259-1 **$16.99**

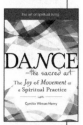

Running—The Sacred Art: Preparing to Practice *by Dr. Warren A. Kay; Foreword by*
Kristin Armstrong 5½ x 8½, 160 pp, Quality PB, 978-1-59473-227-0 **$16.99**

The Sacred Art of Chant: Preparing to Practice
by Ana Hernández 5½ x 8½, 192 pp, Quality PB, 978-1-59473-036-8 **$15.99**

The Sacred Art of Fasting: Preparing to Practice
by Thomas Ryan, CSP 5½ x 8½, 192 pp, Quality PB, 978-1-59473-078-8 **$15.99**

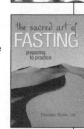

The Sacred Art of Forgiveness: Forgiving Ourselves and Others through God's Grace
by Marcia Ford 8 x 8, 176 pp, Quality PB, 978-1-59473-175-4 **$18.99**

The Sacred Art of Listening: Forty Reflections for Cultivating a Spiritual Practice
by Kay Lindahl; Illus. by Amy Schnapper 8 x 8, 160 pp, b/w illus., Quality PB, 978-1-893361-44-7 **$16.99**

The Sacred Art of Lovingkindness: Preparing to Practice
by Rabbi Rami Shapiro; Foreword by Marcia Ford 5½ x 8½, 176 pp, Quality PB, 978-1-59473-151-8 **$16.99**

Sacred Attention: A Spiritual Practice for Finding God in the Moment
by Margaret D. McGee 6 x 9, 144 pp, Quality PB, 978-1-59473-291-1 **$16.99**

Soul Fire: Accessing Your Creativity
by Thomas Ryan, CSP 6 x 9, 160 pp, Quality PB, 978-1-59473-243-0 **$16.99**

Spiritual Adventures in the Snow: Skiing & Snowboarding as Renewal for Your Soul
by Dr. Marcia McFee and Rev. Karen Foster; Foreword by Paul Arthur
5½ x 8½, 208 pp, Quality PB, 978-1-59473-270-6 **$16.99**

Thanking & Blessing—The Sacred Art: Spiritual Vitality through Gratefulness
by Jay Marshall, PhD; Foreword by Philip Gulley 5½ x 8½, 176 pp, Quality PB, 978-1-59473-231-7 **$16.99**

Spirituality & Crafts

Beading—The Creative Spirit: Finding Your Sacred Center through the Art of Beadwork *by Rev. Wendy Ellsworth*
Invites you on a spiritual pilgrimage into the kaleidoscope world of glass and color. 7 x 9, 240 pp, 8-page color insert, 40+ b/w photos and 40 diagrams, Quality PB, 978-1-59473-267-6 **$18.99**

Contemplative Crochet: A Hands-On Guide for Interlocking Faith and Craft *by Cindy Crandall-Frazier; Foreword by Linda Skolnik*
Illuminates the spiritual lessons you can learn through crocheting.
7 x 9, 208 pp, b/w photos, Quality PB, 978-1-59473-238-6 **$16.99**

The Knitting Way: A Guide to Spiritual Self-Discovery
by Linda Skolnik and Janice MacDaniels Examines how you can explore and strengthen your spiritual life through knitting.
7 x 9, 240 pp, b/w photos, Quality PB, 978-1-59473-079-5 **$16.99**

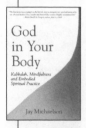

The Painting Path: Embodying Spiritual Discovery through Yoga, Brush and Color *by Linda Novick; Foreword by Richard Segalman*
Explores the divine connection you can experience through art.
7 x 9, 208 pp, 8-page color insert, plus b/w photos, Quality PB, 978-1-59473-226-3 **$18.99**

The Quilting Path: A Guide to Spiritual Discovery through Fabric, Thread and Kabbalah *by Louise Silk*
Explores how to cultivate personal growth through quilt making.
7 x 9, 192 pp, b/w photos and illus., Quality PB, 978-1-59473-206-5 **$16.99**

The Scrapbooking Journey: A Hands-On Guide to Spiritual Discovery
by Cory Richardson-Lauve; Foreword by Stacy Julian Reveals how this craft can become a practice used to deepen and shape your life.
7 x 9, 176 pp, 8-page color insert, plus b/w photos, Quality PB, 978-1-59473-216-4 **$18.99**

The Soulwork of Clay: A Hands-On Approach to Spirituality
by Marjory Zoet Bankson; Photos by Peter Bankson
Takes you through the seven-step process of making clay into a pot, drawing parallels at each stage to the process of spiritual growth.
7 x 9, 192 pp, b/w photos, Quality PB, 978-1-59473-249-2 **$16.99**

Kabbalah / Enneagram
(Books from Jewish Lights Publishing, SkyLight Paths' sister imprint)

Cast in God's Image: Discover Your Personality Type Using the Enneagram and Kabbalah
by Rabbi Howard A. Addison, PhD 7 x 9, 176 pp, Quality PB, 978-1-58023-124-4 **$16.95**

Ehyeh: A Kabbalah for Tomorrow *by Rabbi Arthur Green, PhD*
6 x 9, 224 pp, Quality PB, 978-1-58023-213-5 **$18.99**

The Enneagram and Kabbalah, 2nd Edition: Reading Your Soul
by Rabbi Howard A. Addison, PhD 6 x 9, 192 pp, Quality PB, 978-1-58023-229-6 **$16.99**

The Gift of Kabbalah: Discovering the Secrets of Heaven, Renewing Your Life on Earth
by Tamar Frankiel, PhD 6 x 9, 256 pp, Quality PB, 978-1-58023-141-1 **$16.95**

God in Your Body: Kabbalah, Mindfulness and Embodied Spiritual Practice
by Jay Michaelson 6 x 9, 272 pp, Quality PB, 978-1-58023-304-0 **$18.99**

Jewish Mysticism and the Spiritual Life: Classical Texts, Contemporary Reflections
Edited by Dr. Lawrence Fine, Dr. Eitan Fishbane and Rabbi Or N. Rose
6 x 9, 256 pp, HC, 978-1-58023-434-4 **$24.99**

Kabbalah: A Brief Introduction for Christians
by Tamar Frankiel, PhD 5½ x 8½, 208 pp, Quality PB, 978-1-58023-303-3 **$16.99**

Zohar: Annotated & Explained *Translation & Annotation by Daniel C. Matt; Foreword by Andrew Harvey* 5½ x 8½, 176 pp, Quality PB, 978-1-893361-51-5 **$15.99**

Women's Interest

Women, Spirituality and Transformative Leadership
Where Grace Meets Power
Edited by Kathe Schaaf, Kay Lindahl, Kathleen S. Hurty, PhD, and Reverend Guo Cheen
A dynamic conversation on the power of women's spiritual leadership and its
emerging patterns of transformation. 6 x 9, 288 pp, Hardcover, 978-1-59473-313-0 **$24.99**

Spiritually Healthy Divorce: Navigating Disruption with Insight & Hope
by Carolyne Call A spiritual map to help you move through the twists and turns of
divorce. 6 x 9, 224 pp, Quality PB, 978-1-59473-288-1 **$16.99**

New Feminist Christianity: Many Voices, Many Views
Edited by Mary E. Hunt and Diann L. Neu
Insights from ministers and theologians, activists and leaders, artists and liturgists
who are shaping the future. Taken together, their voices offer a starting point for
building new models of religious life and worship.
6 x 9, 384 pp, HC, 978-1-59473-285-0 **$24.99**

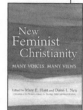

New Jewish Feminism: Probing the Past, Forging the Future
Edited by Rabbi Elyse Goldstein; Foreword by Anita Diamant
Looks at the growth and accomplishments of Jewish feminism and what they mean
for Jewish women today and tomorrow. Features the voices of women from every
area of Jewish life, addressing the important issues that concern Jewish women.
6 x 9, 480 pp, Quality PB, 978-1-58023-448-1 **$19.99**; HC, 978-1-58023-359-0 **$24.99***

Bread, Body, Spirit: Finding the Sacred in Food
Edited and with Introductions by Alice Peck 6 x 9, 224 pp, Quality PB, 978-1-59473-242-3 **$19.99**

Dance—The Sacred Art: The Joy of Movement as a Spiritual Practice
by Cynthia Winton-Henry 5½ x 8½, 224 pp, Quality PB, 978-1-59473-268-3 **$16.99**

Daughters of the Desert: Stories of Remarkable Women from Christian, Jewish
and Muslim Traditions
by Claire Rudolf Murphy, Meghan Nuttall Sayres, Mary Cronk Farrell, Sarah Conover and Betsy Wharton
5½ x 8½, 192 pp, Illus., Quality PB, 978-1-59473-106-8 **$14.99** Inc. reader's discussion guide

The Divine Feminine in Biblical Wisdom Literature
Selections Annotated & Explained
Translation & Annotation by Rabbi Rami Shapiro; Foreword by Rev. Cynthia Bourgeault, PhD
5½ x 8½, 240 pp, Quality PB, 978-1-59473-109-9 **$16.99**

Divining the Body: Reclaim the Holiness of Your Physical Self
by Jan Phillips 8 x 8, 256 pp, Quality PB, 978-1-59473-080-1 **$18.99**

Honoring Motherhood: Prayers, Ceremonies & Blessings
Edited and with Introductions by Lynn L. Caruso
5 x 7¼, 272 pp, Quality PB, 978-1-58473-384-0 **$9.99**; HC, 978-1-59473-239-3 **$19.99**

Next to Godliness: Finding the Sacred in Housekeeping
Edited by Alice Peck 6 x 9, 224 pp, Quality PB, 978-1-59473-214-0 **$19.99**

ReVisions: Seeing Torah through a Feminist Lens
by Rabbi Elyse Goldstein 5½ x 8½, 224 pp, Quality PB, 978-1-58023-117-6 **$16.95***

The Triumph of Eve & Other Subversive Bible Tales
by Matt Biers-Ariel 5½ x 8½, 192 pp, Quality PB, 978-1-59473-176-1 **$14.99**

White Fire: A Portrait of Women Spiritual Leaders in America
by Malka Drucker; Photos by Gay Block 7 x 10, 320 pp, b/w photos, HC, 978-1-893361-64-5 **$24.95**

Woman Spirit Awakening in Nature: Growing Into the Fullness of Who You Are
by Nancy Barrett Chickerneo, PhD; Foreword by Eileen Fisher
8 x 8, 224 pp, b/w illus., Quality PB, 978-1-59473-250-8 **$16.99**

Women of Color Pray: Voices of Strength, Faith, Healing, Hope and Courage
Edited and with Introductions by Christal M. Jackson
5 x 7¼, 208 pp, Quality PB, 978-1-59473-077-1 **$15.99**

The Women's Torah Commentary: New Insights from Women Rabbis on the
54 Weekly Torah Portions *Edited by Rabbi Elyse Goldstein*
6 x 9, 496 pp, Quality PB, 978-1-58023-370-5 **$19.99**; HC, 978-1-58023-076-6 **$34.95***

* A book from Jewish Lights, SkyLight Paths' sister imprint

Spirituality

Gathering at God's Table: The Meaning of Mission in the Feast of Faith
By Katharine Jefferts Schori
A profound reminder of our role in the larger frame of God's dream for a restored and reconciled world. 6 x 9, 256 pp, HC, 978-1-59473-316-1 **$21.99**

The Heartbeat of God: Finding the Sacred in the Middle of Everything
by Katharine Jefferts Schori; Foreword by Joan Chittister, OSB
Explores our connections to other people, to other nations and with the environment through the lens of faith. 6 x 9, 240 pp, HC, 978-1-59473-292-8 **$21.99**

A Dangerous Dozen: Twelve Christians Who Threatened the Status Quo but Taught Us to Live Like Jesus
by the Rev. Canon C. K. Robertson, PhD; Foreword by Archbishop Desmond Tutu
Profiles twelve visionary men and women who challenged society and showed the world a different way of living. 6 x 9, 208 pp, Quality PB, 978-1-59473-298-0 **$16.99**

Decision Making & Spiritual Discernment: The Sacred Art of Finding Your Way *by Nancy L. Bieber*
Presents three essential aspects of Spirit-led decision making: willingness, attentiveness and responsiveness. 5½ x 8½, 208 pp, Quality PB, 978-1-59473-289-8 **$16.99**

Laugh Your Way to Grace: Reclaiming the Spiritual Power of Humor
by Rev. Susan Sparks A powerful, humorous case for laughter as a spiritual, healing path. 6 x 9, 176 pp, Quality PB, 978-1-59473-280-5 **$16.99**

Bread, Body, Spirit: Finding the Sacred in Food
Edited and with Introductions by Alice Peck 6 x 9, 224 pp, Quality PB, 978-1-59473-242-3 **$19.99**

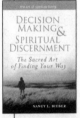

Claiming Earth as Common Ground: The Ecological Crisis through the Lens of Faith
by Andrea Cohen-Kiener; Foreword by Rev. Sally Bingham
6 x 9, 192 pp, Quality PB, 978-1-59473-261-4 **$16.99**

Creating a Spiritual Retirement: A Guide to the Unseen Possibilities in Our Lives
by Molly Srode 6 x 9, 208 pp, b/w photos, Quality PB, 978-1-59473-050-4 **$14.99**

Creative Aging: Rethinking Retirement and Non-Retirement in a Changing World
by Marjory Zoet Bankson 6 x 9, 160 pp, Quality PB, 978-1-59473-281-2 **$16.99**

Keeping Spiritual Balance as We Grow Older: More than 65 Creative Ways to Use Purpose, Prayer, and the Power of Spirit to Build a Meaningful Retirement
by Molly and Bernie Srode 8 x 8, 224 pp, Quality PB, 978-1-59473-042-9 **$16.99**

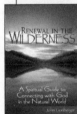

Hearing the Call across Traditions: Readings on Faith and Service
Edited by Adam Davis; Foreword by Eboo Patel
6 x 9, 352 pp, Quality PB, 978-1-59473-303-1 **$18.99**; HC, 978-1-59473-264-5 **$29.99**

Honoring Motherhood: Prayers, Ceremonies & Blessings
Edited and with Introductions by Lynn L. Caruso
5 x 7¼, 272 pp, Quality PB, 978-1-58473-384-0 **$9.99**; HC, 978-1-59473-239-3 **$19.99**

The Losses of Our Lives: The Sacred Gifts of Renewal in Everyday Loss
by Dr. Nancy Copeland-Payton 6 x 9, 192 pp, HC, 978-1-59473-271-3 **$19.99**

Renewal in the Wilderness: A Spiritual Guide to Connecting with God in the Natural World *by John Lionberger*
6 x 9, 176 pp, b/w photos, Quality PB, 978-1-59473-219-5 **$16.99**

Soul Fire: Accessing Your Creativity
by Thomas Ryan, CSP 6 x 9, 160 pp, Quality PB, 978-1-59473-243-0 **$16.99**

A Spirituality for Brokenness: Discovering Your Deepest Self in Difficult Times
by Terry Taylor 6 x 9, 176 pp, Quality PB, 978-1-59473-229-4 **$16.99**

A Walk with Four Spiritual Guides: Krishna, Buddha, Jesus, and Ramakrishna
by Andrew Harvey 5½ x 8½, 192 pp, b/w photos & illus., Quality PB, 978-1-59473-138-9 **$15.99**

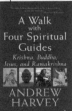

The Workplace and Spirituality: New Perspectives on Research and Practice
Edited by Dr. Joan Marques, Dr. Satinder Dhiman and Dr. Richard King
6 x 9, 256 pp, HC, 978-1-59473-260-7 **$29.99**

Prayer / Meditation

Men Pray: Voices of Strength, Faith, Healing, Hope and Courage
Created by the Editors at SkyLight Paths
Celebrates the rich variety of ways men around the world have called out to the
Divine—with words of joy, praise, gratitude, wonder, petition and even anger—
from the ancient world up to our own day.
5 x 7, 200 pp (est), HC, 978-1-59473-395-6 **$16.99**

Sacred Attention: A Spiritual Practice for Finding God in the Moment
by Margaret D. McGee
Framed on the Christian liturgical year, this inspiring guide explores ways to
develop a practice of attention as a means of talking—and listening—to God.
6 x 9, 144 pp, Quality PB, 978-1-59473-291-1 **$16.99**

Women of Color Pray: Voices of Strength, Faith, Healing, Hope and Courage
Edited and with Introductions by Christal M. Jackson
Through these prayers, poetry, lyrics, meditations and affirmations, you will share
in the strong and undeniable connection women of color share with God.
5 x 7¼, 208 pp, Quality PB, 978-1-59473-077-1 **$15.99**

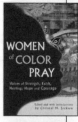

The Art of Public Prayer, 2nd Edition: Not for Clergy Only
by Lawrence A. Hoffman, PhD 6 x 9, 288 pp, Quality PB, 978-1-893361-06-5 **$19.99**

A Heart of Stillness: A Complete Guide to Learning the Art of Meditation
by David A. Cooper 5½ x 8½, 272 pp, Quality PB, 978-1-893361-03-4 **$18.99**

Living into Hope: A Call to Spiritual Action for Such a Time as This
by Rev. Dr. Joan Brown Campbell; Foreword by Karen Armstrong
6 x 9, 208 pp, HC, 978-1-59473-283-6 **$21.99**

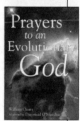

Meditation without Gurus: A Guide to the Heart of Practice
by Clark Strand 5½ x 8½, 192 pp, Quality PB, 978-1-893361-93-5 **$16.95**

Prayers to an Evolutionary God
by William Cleary; Afterword by Diarmuid O'Murchu
6 x 9, 208 pp, HC, 978-1-59473-006-1 **$21.99**

Praying with Our Hands: 21 Practices of Embodied Prayer from the World's
Spiritual Traditions *by Jon M. Sweeney; Photos by Jennifer J. Wilson; Foreword by Mother Tessa
Bielecki; Afterword by Taitetsu Unno, PhD*
8 x 8, 96 pp, 22 duotone photos, Quality PB, 978-1-893361-16-4 **$16.95**

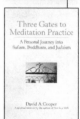

Secrets of Prayer: A Multifaith Guide to Creating Personal Prayer in Your Life
by Nancy Corcoran, CSJ
6 x 9, 160 pp, Quality PB, 978-1-59473-215-7 **$16.99**

Three Gates to Meditation Practice: A Personal Journey into Sufism, Buddhism,
and Judaism *by David A. Cooper* 5½ x 8½, 240 pp, Quality PB, 978-1-893361-22-5 **$16.95**

Prayer / M. Basil Pennington, OCSO

Finding Grace at the Center, 3rd Edition: The Beginning of
Centering Prayer *with Thomas Keating, OCSO, and Thomas E. Clarke, SJ; Foreword by Rev.
Cynthia Bourgeault, PhD* A practical guide to a simple and beautiful form of medita-
tive prayer. 5 x 7¼, 128 pp, Quality PB, 978-1-59473-182-2 **$12.99**

The Monks of Mount Athos: A Western Monk's Extraordinary
Spiritual Journey on Eastern Holy Ground *Foreword by Archimandrite Dionysios*
Explores the landscape, monastic communities and food of Athos.
6 x 9, 352 pp, Quality PB, 978-1-893361-78-2 **$18.95**

Psalms: A Spiritual Commentary *Illus. by Phillip Ratner*
Reflections on some of the most beloved passages from the Bible's most widely
read book. 6 x 9, 176 pp, 24 full-page b/w illus., Quality PB, 978-1-59473-234-8 **$16.99**

The Song of Songs: A Spiritual Commentary *Illus. by Phillip Ratner*
Explore the Bible's most challenging mystical text.
6 x 9, 160 pp, 14 full-page b/w illus., Quality PB, 978-1-59473-235-5 **$16.99**
HC, 978-1-59473-004-7 **$19.99**

About SKYLIGHT PATHS Publishing

SkyLight Paths Publishing is creating a place where people of different spiritual traditions come together for challenge and inspiration, a place where we can help each other understand the mystery that lies at the heart of our existence.

Through spirituality, our religious beliefs are increasingly becoming a part of our lives—rather than *apart* from our lives. While many of us may be more interested than ever in spiritual growth, we may be less firmly planted in traditional religion. Yet, we do want to deepen our relationship to the sacred, to learn from our own as well as from other faith traditions, and to practice in new ways.

SkyLight Paths sees both believers and seekers as a community that increasingly transcends traditional boundaries of religion and denomination—people wanting to learn from each other, *walking together, finding the way.*

For your information and convenience, at the back of this book we have provided a list of other SkyLight Paths books you might find interesting and useful. They cover the following subjects:

Buddhism / Zen	Global Spiritual	Monasticism
Catholicism	Perspectives	Mysticism
Children's Books	Gnosticism	Poetry
Christianity	Hinduism /	Prayer
Comparative	Vedanta	Religious Etiquette
Religion	Inspiration	Retirement
Current Events	Islam / Sufism	Spiritual Biography
Earth-Based	Judaism	Spiritual Direction
Spirituality	Kabbalah	Spirituality
Enneagram	Meditation	Women's Interest
	Midrash Fiction	Worship